GENIUS AND OTHER ESSAYS

GENIUS AND OTHER ESSAYS

BY

EDMUND CLARENCE STEDMAN

KENNIKAT PRESS, INC./PORT WASHINGTON, N. Y.

GENIUS AND OTHER ESSAYS

Copyright 1911 by Moffat, Yard and Co.
Reissued in 1966 by Kennikat Press

Library of Congress Catalog Card No: 66-21388

Analyzed in the ESSAY & GENERAL LITERATURE INDEX

CONTENTS

CONTENTS

EDITORIAL NOTE

For courteous permission to republish these essays we are under obligations to The Houghton Mifflin Company; The Century Company; *The Critic;* The Syndics of the Cambridge University Press, England; Messrs. G. P. Putnam's Sons; Messrs. Henry Holt and Company; Messrs. Charles Scribner's Sons; The King Memorial Committee of the Century Association; and Mr. Richard G. Badger.

LAURA STEDMAN,
GEORGE M. GOULD.

I

GENIUS [1]

A WRITER nowadays hardly makes choice of such a topic as this, unless with due occasion. Even then he leniently recalls the feeling of his schoolboy days, when he sat before a theme—Virtue, Industry, or Ambition—justly out of sorts with his task, if not with his teacher, and much in doubt how to begin it. But I am moved to touch upon the present subject, and in a measure guided, by the striking declaration of one whose original works, no less than his present occupancy of an official chair of criticism, make him a conspicuous authority. No opinion, however striking and unexpected, can fail to receive attention when advanced by Mr. Howells with all his honesty and humor, and in a style so agreeable as to commend him to the favor of even those against whom his gentle shafts of satire are directed.

Not long since, then, our favorite novelist gave a hearing to those who have supported claims, of various parties, to the possession of Genius. He forthwith nonsuited them, on the ground that there was no cause of action. Instead of arguing for an apportionment of the estate indicated by the aforesaid designation,

---

[1] *The New Princeton Review,* September, 1886.

we have, as if claimants to some hypothetical Town-
ley or Hyde inheritance, to face a judicial decision,
based upon evidence satisfactory to the Court at least,
that such a thing does not exist and never has existed.
He finds that there is no such " puissant and admirable
prodigy . . . created out of the common." It is as
much of a superstition as the Maelstrom of Malte-
Brun; it is a mythical and fantastic device, kept up
for the intimidation of modest and overcredulous people. Conformably to this decision, and in frequent
supplementary references thereto, he places the word
" genius " between quotation marks, very much as an
old-time Romanist crossed himself when naming the
Evil One or Oliver Cromwell; or as if it were an im-
postor consigned to the pillory, or a sentenced repro-
bate in charge of a brace of tipstaffs. Mr. Howells's
opinion and practice are of no slight moment. It must
be nothing short of conviction and a sense of duty
that could move him to discredit that of which many
would select himself as an exemplar. Something more
than fair talents, and the aid of the industry which
he celebrates and to which Hercules ever was an ally,
had been required, we thought, to produce those works
of his that give us pride. Should his judgment in time
be reversed,—should the reality of genius be sustained,
after all, then Literature will have reason to exclaim
to him, as La belle Taincturière cried to her jealous
spouse, in *Les Contes Drolatiques: Arrète, malheu-
reux, tu vas tuer le père de tes enfans!*

Sincerity, however, is one of his acknowledged
traits, and none will suspect for an instant that he

would be a willing promulgator of sophistry. That his myth-theory can be, like Bishop Whateley's Napoleon and Mr. Lang's Gladstone, a lively and pleasant bit of by-play, is equally out of the question. Assuming, then, that the popular belief in genius is a superstition, we scarcely can do better than to look into its origin; to inquire whether, like the sun-myth, it is a genuine folk-lore common to all times and races, or something begotten in the romantic passion of the latter-day world. On the whole, I think its adherents may claim for it a respectable antiquity. There are reasons for belief that the Asiatics, with their notions of divination, inspiration, and incarnation, were the progenitors of this tradition, as of so many other fads and fables. But it will suffice to go back to Athens, the distributing reservoir out of which flowed our own stream of thought. From the prince of Grecian idealists we inherit teachings that in the end brought about the use and meaning of our word Genius. With his master, Socrates, he conceived distinctive greatness to be the result of superhuman guidance. To these heathen in their blindness the special power of certain men seemed inexplicable otherwise than as a gift, bestowed by the *daimon*. Plato gossips concerning the etymology of this word, saying that Hesiod uses the title " demons " to denote the " golden race of men who came first," and who, now that fate has closed over the race, are " holy *daimones* upon the earth,—beneficent, averters of ill, guardians of mortal men." In the primitive dialect the word means those who are knowing or wise, and the philosopher avers

that the wise man who happens to be a good man is
daimonion—i.e., more than human. The deduction
finally resulting in our modern illusion was made by
Plato himself, and in various lofty passages. " The
gift," he says in *Ion,* " which you possess of speaking
excellently about Homer, is not an art, but an inspiration: there is a divinity moving in you." Again, the
poet is " a holy thing, and there is no invention in
him until he has been inspired . . . For not by art
does the poet sing, but by power divine." Professor
Jowett's comment inferentially describes genius as
something " unconscious, or spontaneous, or a gift of
nature." Plainly, the Academe and its master should
have a condign share of any criticism to which the
early promoters of this fallacy may be subjected. For
the case of the Jukes affords no plainer evidence of
the spread of wrongful tendencies by multiplication in
descent.

We should have to range through many literatures
to show how this illusion of the Platonists and Neo-
Platonists commended itself to the entire race of philosophers, poets, artists, and warriors, whose vanity
is fed by the conceit that they are a sort of chosen
people. Plutarch made it the final test of his heroes,
and the circle of Augustan wits gave it ready credence.
Cicero declared that all great men were inspired, and
his *furor poeticus* is of a piece with Plato's " divine
frenzy "—whose outcome both deemed far more precious than that of sober reflection. The idea survived
the middle ages, sometimes recurring to its original
and unsophisticated form; but the learned and power-

ful, who had outgrown the pious faith of their ancestors, thought Tasso mad (as indeed he may have been) when he claimed that he was indebted to communication with a familiar spirit for his noblest lyrical discourse, and for that heroic melancholy which, it was said, " raised and brightened his spirit, so far it was from depressing or rendering it obscure." Lord Bacon, certainly a judge of evidence, and one who subjected most things to scientific test, threw the great weight of his authority in favor of the belief that poets and other originators produce by a kind of exceptional gift, if not through direct inspiration. To be sure, he lived in a superstitious time, and put faith, despite his wisdom, in certain mysteries of the quacks and alchemists, in barbarous therapeutic concoctions, and was not wholly incredulous of witchcraft and astrology. He charges a man to set hours for his routine labors, but " whatsoever is agreeable to his nature, let him take no care for any set times; for his thoughts will fly to it of themselves." He conceived that a painter to " make a better face than ever was . . . must do it by a kind of felicity (as a musician that maketh an excellent air in music) and not by rule." Sidney had described poesy as that which " lifts the mind from the dungeon of the body to the enjoying its own divine essence;" and on like ground Bacon thought it partook of divineness, " because it doth raise and erect the mind, by submitting the shews of things to the desires of the mind; whereas reason doth buckle and bow the mind unto the nature of things."

Dryden was one of the earliest English writers to

use the very word genius in the sense of that which
is "the gift of Nature" and which "must be born,
and never can be taught." Its most frequent use by
the Latins was in the sense of a tutelar spirit, but
sometimes, as in Juvenal and Martial, it denoted the
fire of individual greatness. The idea of a divine ad-
monisher was more or less current with the Latins as
with the Greeks. They named this spirit the "inborn,"
and Genius thus came to mean the inspiration rather
than the inspirer, agreeably to the feeling that the soul
is itself divine and its own monitor. In modern times
the word, very slightly inflected, has been more widely
received into European languages, to express a meaning common to all, than almost any other Latin derivative; it is not only found in all Latin tongues,—Italian,
Spanish, Portuguese, French,—but has been adopted
by the Germans, Danes, Swedes, Norwegians, and
other peoples who, like ourselves, have no indigenous
word that conveys precisely the same idea. A universal word means a universal thought. Prophets,
mystics, all direct-inspirationists, still cherish the ger-
minal belief, so rapturously manifest in Jacob Böhme's
avowal: "I say before God that I do not myself know
how it happens to me that, without having the impelling will, I do not know what I should write. For
when I write the Spirit dictates to me." But genius,
in the derivative sense, is equally recognized, the world
over, as a *gift*, something not quite attainable by labor,
however promotive that may be of its bravest exercise,
and a gift of types as various as are the different persons endowed with it.

That this view, however specious, has been captivating to the Teutonic mind, appears not alone from the language of German poets and artists, with their traditional pretensions to the gift, but even more from that of philosophers and critics, having the true father of German criticism at their head. Lessing, the most revolutionary and constructive of critics, the inspirer of creative intellect, reverenced by the youthful Goethe, the guide of Schiller, and accepted by the distrustful Heine within our own time as the paragon of all literary history, even the noble Lessing corporated this vagary into his system, and defends it with fine irony in the *Dramaturgie:*

"To the man of Genius (*Genie*) it is granted not to know a thousand things which every schoolboy knows. . . . He goes wrong, therefore, now from confidence, now from pride, sometimes intentionally, sometimes unintentionally,—so often, so grossly, that we cannot express our wonder enough to other good people. We stand in amazement, clap our hands, and exclaim: ' But how could so great a man be so ignorant? How is it possible it did not occur to him? Did he not reflect, then?' Oh! let us be silent; we think we humiliate him, and only make ourselves ridiculous in his eyes. Everything we know better than he only proves that we went more diligently to school than he; but, unfortunately, that was necessary if we were not to continue perfect blockheads."

He audaciously removes the world of a genius (*die Welt eines Genies*) from the commonplace world at the service of every man. Its events,

" Although they are not of this world, might nevertheless belong to another world— . . . in short, to the world of a genius who (let it be allowed to me to indicate the Creator without name by his noblest creature!), imitating on a small scale the highest Genius (*höchste Genie*), places, exchanges, diminishes, enlarges the parts of the present world in order to make from it a whole of his own with which he connects his own aims."

Elsewhere, while insisting upon the independence of the gift-possessor, he cautions us against the blunder of mistaking pleasure and facility for genius. Lessing, be it observed, classed himself as outside the sacred circle; although his poems and dramas had some vogue, he thought them the outcome of taste and industry, but acknowledged that to criticism he " owed something which comes very near genius." " Otherwise," he wrote, " I do not feel in me the living fountain which works upward by its own force, shoots up by its own force in such rich, fresh, and pure streams. I must force everything out of me by the fly-press and pipes." Yet his biographer says that his insight as a critic was to a large extent " due to the study of his own intellectual processes as a poet." Goethe, a savant and usually possessed of the clearest sense, shared in Lessing's aberration and resisted even the conventional language that tends to rectify it. He would not have it said that Mozart had *composed* Don Juan, but thus assured Eckermann:

" It is a spiritual creation, in which the details, as well as the whole, are pervaded by *one* spirit, and by the truth of *one* life; so that the producer did not make experiments, and patch together, and follow his own caprice, but was altogether in the power of the dæmonic spirit of his genius, and acted according to its orders."

The great writers, mystics and iconoclasts alike, upon whose works our present generation fed in youth, have been subject to this hallucination. There is scarcely an exception in the group of English worthies just prior to our own period of the colored photograph, cast-iron architecture, law as a business, and of book-making as a staple, time-regulated, and surely productive trade. All strike the key of De Quincey's rhapsody on Shakespeare: "O mighty poet! Thy works are not as those of other men, simply and merely great works of art; but are also like the phenomena of nature, like the sun and the sea, the stars and the flowers." It is true that Carlyle, with his varying treatment of prerogative, once or twice made outbursts that have encouraged others to rise, like the poor wise man in the legend, and say: "I doubt!" As we read Mr. Howells's protest, it perforce calls to mind the highest authority citable in its support. Yes, Carlyle wrote that genius "means transcendent capacity of taking trouble, first of all." And he apostrophizes one of his heroes, enduring the discipline of youth:

"Daily return the quiet dull duties. . . . Patience, young man of genius, as the Newspapers would now call you; it is indispensably beneficial nevertheless! To swallow one's disgusts, and do faithfully the ugly commanded

work, taking no counsel with flesh and blood: know that
' genius,' everywhere in Nature, means this first of all."

But Carlyle here reverts to the dogged apprenticeship of " slow, stubborn, broad-shouldered " Friedrich
Wilhelm, and elsewhere he finds something else more
needful than patience first of all: everywhere, one
might say, since of latter-day Englishmen, this chief
exorciser and cloud-dispeller seems from youth to age
to have welcomed most unreservedly the chimera of
genius and to account its exemplars as a select and
consecrated race. To him they are ever the " chosen
men of the world," in all fields of discovery, thought,
action, creative art. In Goethe he salutes " the existence of a high and peculiar genius." His Mirabeau
illustrates the difference " between an original man,
of never such questionable sort, and the most dexterous
cunningly-devised parliamentary mill." The devia-
tions of Richter's star only assure him that " Genius
has privileges of its own; it selects an orbit for itself;
and be this never so eccentric, if it is indeed a celestial
orbit, we mere star-gazers must at last compose ourselves, must cease to cavil at it, and begin to observe
its laws."

Nevertheless, that outbreak of Carlyle's, reënforced
by epigrams attributed to George Eliot and other contemporaries, and of which Mr. Howells gives us the
latest paraphrase, was not lost upon our working-day
and matter-of-fact generation. It was indeed as when
some bold explorer sailed at last between Moskenaes
and Mosken, sounding and heaving his log, and found

a sturdy industrious current, but no Maelstrom supernatural or otherwise. Or it was the jet of cold water
thrown into the boiling, bubbling cauldron and reduc-
ing in a jiffy its superfluous steam. The fire may
still be underneath, and the steam-gauge yet rise high
as ever, but safety and low pressure is the watchword
of a popular engineer. Some of our most brilliant
thinkers, to whom the public would not gainsay the attributes of genius, are quite disenchanted, and recognize it neither in themselves nor in others. The lack
of self-consciousness, however, proves nothing. Carlyle, appropriating Richter's phrase, said that " genius
is ever a secret to itself," and instanced Shakespeare,
" who takes no airs for writing *Hamlet* or *The Tempest,* understands not that it is anything surprising."
But the leader-loving masses have so long eaten of the
insane root that at this moment, as throughout the
centuries, they discern, or believe they discern, the ex-
ceptionally great as plainly as they can distinguish
Sirius and Aldebaran from the multitude of points
that twinkle about them.

I have refrained from looking chiefly among the
poets for qualified judges in the present hearing, for
we shall see that they would be objected to as interested parties, if not peremptorily appealed from, by
the other side. Yet it may be noted that, at about the
time when Mr. Howells rendered his decision, an
American poet, of high critical jurisdiction, was accepting this traditional verity of genius as sound under
the law. In the discourse upon Gray, with which Mr.
Lowell favored the readers of the *New Princeton,* he

said in his unrivalled way that Addison and Steele " together made a man of genius," and drew a fine distinction when he showed that only the vivid genius of Pope could so nearly persuade wit to become poetry. In speaking of the rare, yet occasional, union of genius and dilettantism in the same person, he sees that " genius implies always a certain fanaticism of temperament, which, if sometimes it seems fitful, is yet capable of intense energy on occasion." That which idealizes commonplace, he elsewhere looks upon as "a divine gift," for which to be thankful. If Lowell, too, be mad in this belief, he gives us a sane and luminous exposition of his reasons for it. But one might cite a cloud of other witnesses to prove how ancient, how continuous, how modern, is this instinctive and transmitted obliquity of the noblest minds. Of a truth the one universal foible of men born great —the most striking illustration, possibly, that could strengthen Disraeli's display of the Infirmities of Genius—is their faith in the entity, the actual existence, of a quality by which they still are classified.

That something does exist, something by which great and original things are done, Mr. Howells no less recognizes. Only it is not genius. There must be no titles in the democracies of art, invention, statesmanship, actions, and affairs. As the Terrorists changed St. Matthew's Day to the Fifth Sans-culottide, so genius shall be reduced after this fashion:

" There is no ' genius,' there is only the mastery that comes to natural aptitude from the hardest study of

any art or science." This is his dilution of, or pro-
posed substitute for, the word he consigns to an Index
Expurgatorius. The mooted difference between talent
and genius should no longer distress " poor little au-
thorlings." Genius is the Maelstrom of literary chart-
mongers. The Norwegian Maelstrom within the memory of middle-aged men " existed in the belief of the
geographers, but we now get on perfectly well without it."

With the timidity of an old graduate who tries to
quote Horace before those trained in the latest Roman
pronunciation, I confess myself not wholly free from
the superstition: the scales have not quite dropped
from my own eyes. I have a certain respect for inherited, confirmed proverbs, phrases, and terms; and
it is hard to rid one's self of the feeling that there must
be something in an idea, a judgment, accepted by the
many and the few and from generation to generation,
—there must be some mission for a word which, although it be " soiled with all ignoble use," I find taken
into service, and in a sense differing from talent, or
mastery, or aptitude, by every English writer from
Dryden to Messrs. Gosse and Courthope. I plead
guilty to the charge of having employed it more than
once in consideration of Browning and Tennyson and
Swinburne, of Poe and Emerson, of other exceptional
singers in our time. Indeed, I do not see how we can
get on without it until some apter term is proffered to
embody what seems a distinct idea. Mr. Howells's
paraphrase may serve for a definition, if you give it a
superlative and intense force, a moral ictus a hundred

times more impressive than that which it conveys to the unprepared reader. Natural aptitude, of a truth— but aptitude so unique, so compelling, as to have seemed supernatural to the ancients, preternatural to the common folk of all times, prenatal and culminative to the scientific observer of heredity, evolution, environment. Having progressed from the "wit" of our English forefathers to this expressive "genius," shall we go back to "natural aptitude" forsooth? If we must have a paraphrase, let us resort to the essential and basic salt rather than to a triturated and hyper-reduced solution. I would rather seek for it, at the other extreme, in some extravagant gloria of Carlyle's *Past and Present:*

"Genius, Poet, do we know what these words mean? An inspired Soul once more vouchsafed to us, direct from Nature's own fire-heat, to see the Truth, and speak it and do it."

"Genius is the 'inspired gift of God.' It is the clearer presence of God Most High in a man. Dim, potential, in all men, in this man it has become actual. So says John Milton, who ought to be a judge; so answer him the Voices of all Ages and all Worlds."

I would not dispute about words, and am quite aware that Carlyle's other view may constitute a ground for appeal to Philip sober. And I am equally aware how far his "infinite capacity for taking trouble" has echoed and extended,—until it has become almost a cult with men less authoritative than its latest transmitter, and given what infinite comfort to steady plodders, men of system, industry, and—for once let us say—talent, to whom after all the world is diurnally indebted!

Yet even the avowed promoters of this reform at times betray an unconscious or subjective distrust of it. I once heard a master of the art preservative of arts, as he scouted the popular notion of genius. With good mental and bodily powers, he said, it needs no special gift, nothing but industry and a fair chance, to put one at the head of any art or science—to produce the exact results which the lazy and credulous attribute to distinctive faculty. The company present questioned this, suggesting that the test be applied to specific cases. The painter, who in childhood drew with ease the likenesses of his playmates, and afterwards rose to greatness, had he not an innate gift that no industry and training could rival? The musician, seemingly born with musical ear and voice, or with instinctive mastery of instruments,—the inventor, the romancer,—was there nothing unique and exceptional in their capabilities? No, our sturdy friend replied— he would not own that any man of general ability could not equally perfect his eye and hand, ear and voice, by thorough devotion and practice. To a man who so cheerfully disposed of these extreme illustrations there was really no reply. But within ten minutes, conversation having changed to the subject of typography and book-making, he gratified us with some account of his own experience while advancing an art in which he deservedly stands at the front. We expressed our admiration for his achievements, and

for his natural taste; whereupon he modestly said that
he believed he had a genius for printing, that he was
born to be a printer,—not reflecting, until the phrases
had slipped from him, that he inadvertently refuted
his previous argument. We assured him that he was
right—he *had* a genius for printing, and had not the
art been in existence, his life would have been as imperfect as that of many a ne'er-do-well before the
Civil War revealed that he was born to be a fighter
and hero. Here we again reach the primal attribute
of what the world, in its simplicity, denominates
genius: it is *inborn,* not alone with respect to bodily
dexterity and the fabric of the brain, but as apper-
taining to the power and bent of the soul itself. Channing went so far as to claim that Milton's command
of harmony is not to be ascribed to his musical ear:
" It belongs to the soul. It is a gift or exercise of
genius, which has power to impress itself on whatever
it touches, and finds or frames, in sounds, notions,
and material forms, correspondences and harmonies
with its own fervid thoughts and feelings." This does
not conflict with a scientific diagnosis, as we shall
presently see. Remove the investigation to the domain
of psychology, and the law is still there; we declare
to the most plain-spoken realist that there is nothing
out of nature in it, although our psychology may as
yet be too defective to formulate it. But as nothing
can restrict the liberty of the soul, Channing recognized the freedom of genius to choose its own language and its own working-law.

A debate once arose, in my hearing, upon the question: Which of two virtuous men is the better, he whose virtue is ingrained and natural, or he who, born with evil traits, has educated and disciplined himself to virtue? A youth spoke up for the latter as having the higher order of goodness. But he was rebuked by an elderly man, who said that the latter in truth might be the more praiseworthy for self-control, but asked if it was to be supposed that man could excel the Creator in fashioning character? He added that a person made good at the outset by the Master Workman, and thus good by nature, is not liable to decline; that his goodness is a constant, self-dependent factor, while the goodness attained by effort is variable, and must be watched incessantly and maintained by fresh effort, and, as in the case of Doctor Dodd, whose over-acquisitiveness at last got the better of him, is liable to give way at any moment of relaxed vigilance. Thus it may be, I should think, that genius demands and gains an admiration not excited by mere aptness strengthened through " taking trouble " and " the hardest study." Like beauty, it is its own excuse for being. Its claim to special honor is all the more indisputable if Florus was sound in his maxim—*Poeta nascitur, non fit.*

It would seem, furthermore, that there is genius, and genius. First, the puissant union of divers forces that has made rare " excepted souls " great in various directions, foremost and creative in every work to which they set themselves. Names of these, the world's few, are ever repeated—such as Cæsar, Peter the Great, Michael Angelo, Bacon, Goethe—men of combined powers, and among them we always class Shake-speare—poet, manager, citizen—because his writings reflect mankind at large and we justly call him the myriad-minded. If our Franklin had possessed more ideality, he clearly, despite the counter-assumption of Mr. Howells, would rank with the second order of this class. The more limited kind of genius, and that most speedily and easily recognized by the world, is the *specific*. Its possessor is born with an irrepressible faculty for some distinctive labor, art, or science. It belongs to your poets, romancers, artists, inventors, etc.—Æschylus, Pheidias, Dante, Cervantes, Rabelais, Newton, Haller, Pitt, Hannibal, Nelson; to Keats and Burns and Byron, Thackeray and Dickens; to Kean, Rachel, Bernhardt; to the Ericssons and Edisons, even to the Zerah Colburns, Morphys, and other representatives of special and more or less abnormal powers. In one case a single point of light requires all the dynamic force of its displayer to sustain it; others reach a good average development in many ways. Again, the genius of each class has its subdivisions— this poet or painter is sublime—this other notable for beauty, or pathos, or delicacy. Thus the element of *personality* is to be considered; the product of special genius always having distinct and individual flavor. Nothing before or after exactly fills its place. De Quincey says, with regard to Milton, that " if the man had failed, the power would have failed. In that mode of power which he wielded, the function was ex-hausted in the man—species was identified with the individual—the poetry was incarnated in the poet."

[18]

In high potencies of this specific genius, the function
is as clearly differentiated as that which marks the
greyhound for speed, the bloodhound for scent, the
bull-dog for grip and combativeness.

Of course it is by an extreme instance that the existence of such a thing as innate and special genius can
be most easily, yet no less fairly, illustrated. Take
the case of that born musician—if there ever is one—
of whom it has been said that "the whole of music
created since Guido d'Arezzo, who invented the musical signs, up to the end of the last century, had only
one aim—to create Mozart." From his letters, and
from the collected anecdotes of his radiant career, a
wealth of undisputable evidence is at hand, almost
justifying this high-flown statement. It has a scientific countenance in certain facts—that his father was
a musician; that Mozart was bred in the service of
a cathedral choir; that he came just at the time when
Gluck "had given impulse and reform to opera," and
Handel and Bach had advanced music to the stage
required for the fit exercise of his transcendent gift.
But the gift itself! So transcendent, so inborn, that
the child must have seemed a changeling, first cradled
in the shell of Apollo's lyre. We are told that when
Wolfgang was three years old he searched out thirds
on the piano; when four, he began playing,—at five,
composing,—at six, he was a celebrity. His *Opus I.,*
four sonatas for piano and violin, was produced when
he was seven. A biographer, describing his fourth
year, says that his faculty was intuitive, " for in
learning to play he learned to compose at the same

time, his own nature discovering to him some important secrets in melody, rhythm, and the art of setting a bass." When he heard discordant sounds, he turned pale and fell into convulsions,—like some modern realist chancing to overhear such words as romance, genius, poet. He was deemed a phenomenon; his aptitude was creative, his youthful mastery not the result of much practice. A man at the piano, organ, violin, harpsichord, he was a frolicsome child the moment his passion left him. The awakening of his heart, when he became a lover, intensified his musical work. Otherwise he remained, in certain respects, always a child; his gift did not imply greatness in many directions, it was his chief mode of expression—he used it because he must, even though it kept him in penury. In music he progressed steadily through life, despite his precocity, and to such effect that his compeers, lamenting his early death, also felt relieved, for while Mozart lived, well might Hasse exclaim: *Questo ragazzo ci farè dimanticar tutti!* Here, then, was one personage equipped, apparently at birth, with the aural, manual, emotional, and creative genius for the expression of a human soul in music.

The case of Mozart leads to the final path of our inquiry, perhaps the only one that will be acknowledged as worth attention in this analytic and scrutinizing age. Thus far, referring to the dogmatic claims of idealists since Plato's time, we have been forced to bear in mind that this inherited conception of genius may be a prolonged illusion. But now the most penetrative of modern thinkers have subjected it to the test of a stern and ruthless philosophy, to the crucial processes of German ratiocination,—and with what result? They not only admit, but insist upon, its verity; they define it, and declare the method of its working. They enable us to maintain, with some show of courage, that the intuitionists, if not the inspirationists, are right, and that Mr. Howells is wrong. Without the slightest reserve they pronounce genius to be *the activity and efflux of the Intellect freed from the domination of the Conscious Will.*

No writers, in truth, have more dispassionately considered the natures of talent and genius than the pessimist Schopenhauer, and his great living successor, Eduard von Hartmann. In their philosophies, creative faculty and taste are discussed with a beautiful precision rarely displayed by the professed masters of æsthetics. Schopenhauer found talent to lie in the greater skill and acuteness of the discursive than of the intuitive cognition; while genius exhibits a development of the intuitive faculty greater than is needed for the service of the Will.

"What is called the stirrings of genius, the hour of consecration, the moment of inspiration, is nothing but the liberation of the intellect, when the latter, for the time exempt from service to the will . . . is active all alone, of its own accord. . . . Then the intellect is of the greatest purity, and becomes *the true mirror of the world.* . . . In such moments, as it were, the soul of immortal works is begotten."

Here we see why genius is a riddle to itself, conferring benefits unconsciously, even involuntarily. Ruskin declares " there are no laws by which we can write Iliads." Carlyle finds manufacture " intelligible but trivial; creation is great, and cannot be understood." He, too, says that " the Voluntary and Conscious bear a small proportion in all the departments of Life, to the Involuntary and Unconscious." But Hartmann has made the final and definitive exposition of this theorem. He perceives that " ordinary talent produces artificially by means of *rational selection* and combination, guided by its æsthetic judgment, . . . It may accomplish something excellent, but can never attain to anything great . . . nor produce an *original work*. . . . Everything is still done with conscious choice; there is wanting the divine frenzy, the vivifying breath of the Unconscious. . . . Conscious combination may, in course of time, be acquired by effort of the conscious will, by industry, endurance, and practice. The creations of genius are unwilled, passive conception; it does not come with the word, but quite unexpectedly, as if fallen from heaven, on journeys, in the theatre, in conversation, everywhere when it is least expected, always suddenly and instantaneously." [1] He then goes on to show how the conscious combination (of talent) works out laboriously the smallest details, while the conception of genius receives the whole from one mould, as the gift of the gods, unearned by toil; that all this is confirmed by all true geniuses who have given us their self-observa-

---

[1] *Philosophy of the Unconscious.* See the chapter on "The Unconscious in the Æsthetic Judgment and in Artistic Production." English ed. Vol. I, pp. 269-292.

tions, and that every one who ever has had a truly original thought can find it preserved in his own experience. In illustration of these truths, Hartmann also instances Mozart, quoting a most apt passage from a letter in Jahn's biography of the musician:

" What, you ask, is my method? . . . I do not myself know and can never find out. When I am in particularly good condition, perhaps riding in a carriage, or in a walk after a good meal, or in a sleepless night, then the thoughts come to me in a rush, and best of all. *Whence and how—that I do not know and cannot learn. . . . All the finding and making only goes on in me as in a very vivid dream.* . . . What now has thus come into being in this way, that I do not easily forget again, and it is perhaps the best gift which the Lord God has given me."

The last clause is a very profound observation, and one which only a true genius would make. All of us, in certain neurotic crises, hear music or see pictures or receive other striking and mysterious impressions. But the born musician, painter, idealist—these alone have the gift of vividly remembering such impressions and the power to convey them, each in his own way, to the approving world. As a literary counterpart to the experience of Mozart, I will refer to the testimony of Dickens, who certainly had genius, if there be such a gift. He was a seer of visions. " Amid silence and darkness . . he heard voices and saw objects; of which the revived impressions to him had the vividness of sensations, and the images his mind created in explanation of them had the coercive force of realities." Lewes avers that Dickens once declared to him " that every word said by his characters was distinctly heard by him," and this the philosopher explains by a theory of hallucination. But Dickens himself, while suffering illness and sorrow in the darkest hour of his life, wrote to Forster:

" May I not be forgiven for thinking it a wonderful testimony to my being made for my art, that when, in the midst of this trouble and pain, I sit down to my book, some beneficent power shows it all to me, and tempts me to be interested, and *I don't invent it*—really do not—*but see it,* and write it down. . . . It's only when all fades away and is gone, that I begin to suspect that its momentary relief has cost me something."

Special examples of this kind must have brought Schopenhauer to avow that " Genius is a man who knows without learning, and teaches the world what he never learned." Lavater, observing its distinctive individuality, said: " Who can produce what none else can, has genius," and that its proportion to the vulgar is "like one to a million." I may summarize all these reflections by the statement that genius lies in the doing of one thing, or many things, through power resulting from the unconscious action of the free intellect, in a manner unattainable by the conscious effort of ordinary men.

So much for the stress of natural aptitude required to sustain these claims. That this inherent power can display its full capabilities only through industry, only by " taking trouble," the world, quite as well as Mr. Howells, has long been aware. We demand that the Will shall perfect its work, and know that the gift is checked, wasted, or quite thrown away, for want of such an ally. And since the will is conscious or unconscious, so also may be its active force as displayed in study, industry, and production. In youth the will to grow and gain through work is often unconscious, but after culture and experience it applies itself to the extreme utilization of the intuitional. Then the fortunate soul reflects on its own possession, and knows why its creations are good. Then it exclaims with Mozart—" People err if they think my art has cost me no trouble; I assure you, my dear friend, no one has taken such pains with the study of composition as I." And thus the critic justly says of Mozart that effects now hackneyed were, in his works, " the joint production of lofty genius and profound contrapuntal knowledge." Yes, genius will work; it is impelled " to scorn delights and live laborious days." It " cannot else." The fire must out or it will consume its inheritor. Mr. Churchill, in *Kavanagh*, just misses being a genius, because he is not driven to perform his work either at a heat or by rational stages. The story of unconscious self-training ever repeats itself; the childhood of Burns and Keats and Mrs. Browning, of James Watt, has a method of finding the precise nurture suited to it. Of course a poor soil, the absence of sunlight, will starve the plant or warp it to some morbid form. But how gloriously it thrives in its true habitat and at its proper season. Time and the man have fitted each other so happily that many ask—as Mr. Howells asks concerning Grant, Bismarck, Columbus, Darwin, Lincoln—who calls such an one a

[25]

genius? Often, too, as in the cases of at least two of these men, the coincidents are so marked that the actors lose the sense of their own destiny, and imagine themselves chiefly suited to something quite otherwise from the work to which the very stars of heaven have impelled them. But fair aptitude, with ceaseless industry and aspiratioin, never can impose itself for genius upon the world. It will produce Southeys in a romantic period and Trollopes in a realistic one. We see the genius of Poe broken by lack of will, and that of Emily Brontë clouded by a fatal bodily disease; but, as against *Wuthering Heights* with its passionate incompleteness, Trollope's entire product stands for nothing more than an extensive illustration of mechanical work against that which reeks with individuality, and when set against the work of true genius reënforced by purpose, physical strength, and opportunity, as exhibited by Thackeray or Hugo or Dickens, comparison is simply out of thought. Not every mind catches fire with its own friction and emits flashes that surprise itself, as in dreams one is startled at things said to him, though he actually is both interlocutor and answerer. Thus Swift, reading his *Tale of a Tub,* exclaims " Good God! what a genius I had when I wrote that book! " Thackeray confessed his delight with the passage where Mrs. Crawley, for a moment, adores her stupid husband after his one heroic act. " There," cried the novelist, " *is* a stroke of genius! " It was one of the occasions when, like our Autocrat composing " The Chambered Nautilus," he had written " better than he could."

If genius has its fountain in the soul, its impulse must be toward Ideality. It seeks that ideal which is the truest truth, the absolute realism. The poet and novelist do not withdraw themselves from constant study of the world,—that is for the abstract philosopher, as in Phaedo:

" I thought as I had failed in the contemplation of true existence, I ought to be careful that I did not lose the eye of my soul. . . . I was afraid my soul might be blinded altogether if I looked at things with my eyes, or tried to apprehend them by the help of the senses. And I thought I had better have recourse to the world of mind and seek there the truth of existence."

Yet Hartmann is sound in his belief that genius always beholds a different world from the apparent, *" though only by gazing deeper into the one lying before him as well,* because the world is represented in his mind more objective, consequently, purer and clearer." True realism, then, is the basis of creative idealism, and it is narrowness to exclude either from an artist's method, which needs the one for its ground and the other for its glory. Bacon writes of " a more ample greatness, a more exact goodness, and a more absolute variety than can be found in the nature of things." He finds that to be " the best part of beauty which a picture cannot express." The picture or poem that expresses this most nearly is closest to the ideal, and conveys to us, I think, a vivid impression of the gift under discussion. Get down to popular instinct, and you will find a current belief that it is the privilege of genius to see the soul of things; not merely their externals, but to know, to feel, the secret meaning of all that makes up life. Observation, experience, industry, unaided by this highest sense, are of less worth than the service of Paul and Apollos without the heaven-given increase.

This ideal tendency, and the intuitive vision of what is ever real, are revealed both in choice of field and in treatment, however varied these may be by time, situation, and the workman's personality. Real life includes the commonplace—it never yet was confined to it. Creations of the first order, though out of common experience, seem usual and among the verities, and this because nature is what must be depicted, and not alone in its superficial, every-day guises. We find nothing improbable in the most fantastic or ethereal conceptions of Cervantes, Shakespeare, Spenser—the world of their imaginings is a real world. They do not conflict with the " sanity of true genius," of which Lamb says that, where it seems most to recede from humanity, it will be found the truest to it. " Herein," he adds, " the great and little wits are differenced, . . . if the latter wander ever so little from nature or actual existence, they lose themselves and their readers."

If this should by chance be true, if all these thinkers have not been quite distraught, then the difference between a vital realism and that which we outlive and outgrow is not, as Mr. Howells puts it with respect to genius, a difference " in degree." It is the difference between radical and superficial methods, between insight and outsight—between work by men who have the gift, and that by plodding yet complacent crafts-men with no intensity of " natural aptitude " and no " mastery " that can rank them with the masters. I do not think realism a modern discovery, whether French, English, or American; it has been manifest equally in romantic and common-sense periods, and just as true to nature in select and noble types as in those which are irreclaimably provincial or vulgar. The works of Thackeray, not excepting *Henry Es-mond*, are as realistic as those of Trollope or of the most uncompromising Zolaites. They are more so, because more elevated, and more intense in their ex-quisite portrayal of life's varied forms. Even to con-vey instruction you must stir the soul—the lesson that was not felt is soon forgotten.

But to do this, two things are essential, traits which this so-called genius ever has been observed to possess in a notable degree. The higher realism depends upon Imagination for the genesis of its ideal. It is imag-ination that makes study of external things, and con-ceives of novel and more perfect and exciting uses and combinations that may be made of them—without transcending the limits of nature. The second thing required is Passion—resolving, annealing, sympathetic —that comprehends and can excite the strongest feel-ing of which our lives are capable. Genius is thought to be creative, because it imagines clearly, and to lay hold upon us by the passionate intensity from which the world gathers a responsive heat.

It is a natural inference that writers who labor to

disenthrall us from the nympholepsy and illusions of
the past, who deprecate any rehearsal of emotions
keyed above the level every-day scale, who turn by
choice to unheroic and matter-of-fact life, and believe
that one theme or situation is as good as another,
provided it be honestly elaborated—it is to be inferred,
I say, that such writers must come to distrust the value
of any intellectual power which tends to ideality, and
makes choice instinctively of a stimulating treatment
and an ideal theme. One may expect them to doubt
even the existence of that high faculty which answers
the heart's desire for what is imaginative, stirring—
romantic, if you choose; which depicts forcibly because
it feels intensely, and which moreover, as if through
inspiration, masters its field without the painful study
to which they devote themselves, and with the careless
felicity of nature itself. Nor are they quite without
justification. The photographic method has its use—
no realism can be too faithful in the description of matters excellent and beautiful in themselves. But with
discourse and materials that are essentially vulgar
or distasteful, and not even picturesque in studies, the
result is scarcely worth attaining. There is a quali-
tative meanness in the pantry-talk and key-hole dis-
closures of *Lovell the Widower,* Thackeray's nearest
descent to this kind of work. Why should we be led
of malice aforethought in creative art—of which poetry and the novel may be taken as types—to the
persistent contemplation of boorish and motiveless
weaklings, although they swarm about us, and add to
the daily weariness of humdrum life? Even the

knaves, proletarians, adventurers, that genius creates, interest us and are ideal in their way. But apply the detective's method to the movements and gabble of doughy nonentities, and a conviction soon arises in the public mind that an author's reliance upon the phonograph and pocket-camera may be carried too long and too far.

It is against the poets that our novelist-critic finally reveals a special and Junonian grudge. For, is it not that the poets, " having most of the say in this world, abuse it to shameless self-flattery "? Do they not set up this prerogative of " genius," and claim it chiefly as their own? Therefore our danger is not a famine, but a gross surfeit, of poets—all claiming to be great, unless the hot gridiron be ready for their broiling. If we are to have no more good bards, so much the better—there will be less ridiculous caracoling on the part of otherwise sensible persons, and less to blush and grieve for. Besides, haven't we still and always the great poets of the past, and haven't they given the world quite as much of the light and charm as is good for it?

To this effect, and more of the like, Mr. Howells; and, in these days of cheap postage for third-class matter, there are men of his profession, haplessly located in the publishing centres, who have even more cause than he to cry—bother the scribblers that bloom in all seasons. To represent the forty thousand post-offices of these reading and writing States there is an equal number of persons, old and young, male and

female, versifiers and prosers, whose genius is of that
sort which Mr. Bronson Howard has defined as " Talent, in the first person singular." These are they who
distress their cockney brother with pleas and commis-
sions such as no proud, self-respecting striver ever
yet stooped to make. They spare him not in his luck
or disaster, health or sickness, leisure or overwork.
Often the scant time which he hopes to devote to his
own vintage is wasted, even if he does no more than
to acknowledge their demands that he shall market, or
at least sample, their too often insipid and watered
grape-juice. Yet the world has always got on after
this fashion. The laureate's reflection on nature, that
of fifty seeds she often brings but one to bear, is an
under-statement. She summons a thousand talesmen
to get even a petty juror. Doubtless an artist, orator,
novelist, or poet, with never so little of the *sang azur,*
belongs to the blood—a trying and unconscionable poor
relation, but still not a commoner—most likely not so
good as a commoner, but let the underlings flout at
him, not the knights and nobles. If such considerations weigh not with the justly prosperous master of
an Editor's Study, he nevertheless will forbear, on
second thought, to wish out of existence this breed
of ready subjects for his merry humor. What adequate relief to toil, what break to official monotony,
if one cannot occasionally lay down the sword of
argument and lance of fellowship, and throw clubs
at the stock butts of one's profession! So thought
the great Dean, in his discourse to prove that " The
abolishing of Christianity " might be attended with

inconveniences. " The gentlemen of wit," he wrote, who are offended by the sight of so many " draggled-tail parsons," do not consider " what an advantage and felicity it is for great wits to be always provided with objects of scorn and contempt, in order to exercise and improve their talents, and divert their spleen from falling on each other or on themselves; especially when all this may be done without the least imaginable danger to their own persons."

Our discourager of poetic fluency, then, will do well to hesitate before quite putting out the class whose writhings under " the question " may yield him further delectation. Nor are they so easily disposed of; minor organizations cling to life. The bardlings may derive much edification from Mr. Howells's little homily, but 'tis doubtful whether threats or Scripture will compel them to forego. St. Anthony preached a notable sermon to the fishes; they never had been so edified, but—

> The sermon now ended,
> Each turned and descended;
> The pikes went on stealing,
> The eels went on eeling;
>   Much delighted were they,
>   But preferred the old way.

Our pastoral pipers, moreover, are not unlikely to challenge their denouncer's consistency. What, they will cry, of your growing tribe of novelists? If the poets, poor and otherwise, are always with us, their ranks seem thin, confronting those of the tale-writers that spring up from the teeth sown by Mr. Howells and his brilliant compeers. "They say he cried out of sack," quoth Nym, discussing the pious end of doughty Sir John. We have mine hostess's word for it that he did *not* cry out upon that dearer foolishness to which he had also been devoted. We need not renew the question whether some who once took to "versing" now take to "noveling" as the fashion of the time—either practice is venial beside that of coining uncouth and felonious words. Mr. Howells remembers a small volume of early verse, and believes that almost any middle-aged literary man can think of another. The present writer, for his part, recalls a certain early novel; yet the fact that, unlike his friend's artistic poetry, it never merited and obtained publication, shall not warp him from his belief that there are good stories yet to be told. But, good as our best novelists are, fresh as is the promise of those arising in many sections, glad as we are of America's prowess in her new field—is her poetry solely white-weed and wild-carrot? Is the novel our only "good grass"? And have the novelists, great and little, all the modesty? We are told that "if we should have no more poets, we might be less glorious as a race, but we certainly should be more modest—or they would." We are asked, "If we are to have no more great poetry, haven't we the great poets of the past inalienably still?" Have there been, then, no great novelists in the past? To speak plainly, the little bard and the little tale-writer seem to me very much like two of a kind. All makers of verse and story of old were classed together, and, as "literary fellows" and en-

couragers of dreams and idleness, were banished from
Plato's Republic. Nor do I see that one class of these
workmen is more modest than another; the modesty
of each is found among true artists of whom Mr.
Howells is an enviable type, and whose best work
seems to them still incomplete. The verse-maker has
an innocent and traditional reverence for his " ideal,"
but a little ideality just now will do no harm. Grace
will be given us to endure it. In fact, the two kinds
of *poiëtæ* can be of mutual service. The poet can
wisely borrow the novelist's lamp of truth, and put
more reason in his rhymes, while the novelist emu-
lates the color and passion of the poet,—so that verse
will be something more than word-music, and the novel
gain in feeling, movement, Life. For life is not insured by a refined adjustment of materials, even though
they display the exact joinery and fitness of the American coat which a New York lawyer, of mellow wit
and learning, proffered as a model to his Bond Street
tailor. " There," said he, " can you, Shears, make
anything like that in London?" "Upon my word,
Mr. M——, I think we should hardly care to, if we
could." "But why not, man? Does it not fit perfectly, is it not cut and sewed perfectly, and are not
all the lines graceful and trim? What does it want?
in what can you excel it? what does it lack?" "Quite
so," mused the tailor, without a trace of assent in his
face; "it does seem to lack something, you know."
"Well, what?" "I beg your pardon, sir; 'tis very
neat work,—a world of pains to it,—but we might say
it lacks—Life!"

[35]

But as for our prime question of the reality of genius, and the legitimate force of a word common to so many literatures, I think that, if the general recognition of these be indeed the effect of an illusion, the Power which shapes human destiny is not yet ready to remove the film from our eyes. Should the world's faith be an ignorant one, I still am so content with this inspiring dream left us in a day of disenchantment as to esteem it folly to be wise. It seems that Mr. Courthope and Mr. Gosse also " talk from time to time " of this phantasmal " something." Do these writers, do I, asks our friendly reviewer, really believe in it? Can they, can I, severally lay hands upon our waistcoats and swear that we think there is any such thing? It would be taking an unfair advantage to interpret this seriously—to assume that he would expect these English gentlemen and scholars perforce to recant, " when upon oath," a declaration made out of court; and for myself, I hope to have grace to confess a change of opinion, and I have no fear that the omission of an oath would greatly lessen his belief in my honesty of statement. But when asked, " is a ' genius ' at all different from other men of like gifts, except in degree?" I reply that this is begging the question. At present, I believe that the other men have not the " like gift," that the difference is one of quality, not of quantity or " degree." The unique gift, the individuality of the faculty or faculties, constitutes the genius.

Mr. Howells rightly lays stress upon the well-known danger, even to a candid mind, of nursing a pet theory.

It is just as unwise for an inventive author, even in a mood of self-analysis, to toy with a theoretical paradox, for literary methods grow by what they feed on. It is not for this, as I have said, that his admirers (and none more than the present writer) are grateful to him; it is for the pleasure derived from very original works, the product of something more creative than even his indomitable labor, and conscientious study of the novelist's craft and properties. One is apt to set too little value upon the gift which is his alone— the faculty that makes so light to him that portion of his work which his fellows cannot master by praying or fasting. He is just as prone, moreover, to regard that as most essential which is hardest for himself, yet necessary to the perfect work, thus setting the labor, wherewith he procures and mixes components, above the one drop of an elixir solely his own, that adds the transmuting spirit to their mass. Our deft student and painter of New England life still has his fairy spectacles—they are not lost, but on his own forehead. Finally, it is a trait of genius, in its method of expression, to discover and avail itself of the spirit of its time. My avowal that Mr. Howells had done this betrayed no savor of the charge of time-serving. It seemed to me, on the contrary, that consciously or unconsciously he had obeyed the ancient oracle, and that the admonition *Follow thy Genius* had left its impress upon his whole career.

II

WHAT IS CRITICISM?[1]

A QUESTION put in this direct way, as if from a text-book, is first of all entitled to a plain and elementary rejoinder, if one can be devised.

I even hope that in time some dialectician, as "absolute" as the Grave-digger in "Hamlet," will hit upon an exact reply to the question, What is Poetry? This so many idealists have failed to answer, because they feel and do not analyze; because they attempt by sentiment and inadequate analogy to produce in us their own feeling, rather than to define what is, after all, a human mode of expression and therefore within man's power to define. Feeling *is* " deeper than all thought," but when the poet Cranch tells us also that " thought is deeper than all speech," he is met by the poet Poe with the confession: " I do not believe that any thought, properly so called, is out of the reach of language. I fancy, rather, that where difficulty in expression is experienced there is, in the intellect which experiences it, a want either of deliberateness or method." He also observes that " the thought is logicalized by the effort at expression." For a dreamer and man of feeling, whose learning was none

¹ *The Epoch*, March 11 and 18, 1887.
[38]

too exact, Poe had a curiously scientific method. His perception of the logic of the beauty which he so adored was always vivid. And his own definition of poetry, though exclusive and narrow, is almost the only one on ·record which conforms to the Euclidean maxim, viz., That a definition shall distinguish the thing defined from all things else.

There is nothing so nebulous in the meaning of Criticism as to befog either its ·practitioners or the logicians. The dictionaries consider it chiefly in its relation to art and letters. For myself, now first attempting to define a function which nearly all modern writers exercise, I can offer no formula which seems more simple and comprehensive than the following:

Criticism is the art and practice of declaring in what degree any work, character or action conforms to the Right.

Conversely, and implied in this definition, the office of criticism is to see and declare what is wrong—*i. e.,* in what degree a work fails to conform to the Right. As " the Right " fully includes certain traditional constituents—the true, the beautiful, the good—the term thus applies to all matters of fact, taste, virtue, all questions, in other words, of verity, æsthetics and morals. Since analysis resolves it in this wise, the primary qualifications of a critic are accuracy, taste and honesty. Assuredly the last two of these should be inborn, and all are heightened by exercise and culture.

In the differentiation of effort we find many critics restricting themselves, or best adapted, to the review of specific arts—often to special subdivisions of an art. But the consensus of the fine arts, for example, is such that, while each has inexorable limits, they all move in harmony and subject to the same enduring principles. The critic then, even in technical examination of a painting, drama, novel or any other artistic structure, must be grounded in general laws and sensible of their application to other forms of creative work than the one under his immediate observation. Just as a specialist in the art of healing—say an oculist—or a physician essaying to cure the slightest ailment, must have a sound knowledge of therapeutics and anatomy. Otherwise his practice will be inconsistent and hazardous.

The ideal critic is one of universal prerogative. His faculty and doctrine, if trustworthy in one direction, can hardly go far astray in the others. Even in æsthetics a thinker, deliberately conscious of beauty, will recognize its correlation with the true and the good. I am skeptical as to the radical inaccuracy or immorality of noted critics and artists who perceive or create what is lastingly beautiful; yet defects of temperament may influence very adversely their personal conduct of life.

The ideal spirit of criticism is pure and high. The declarer of Right, in its various provinces, assumes the office of a censor, a judge, and if he has no innate gift of perception, supported by acquired knowledge, his assumption will be characterized in the invidious sense of the word. He may have his special tastes and leanings, but private considerations have nothing to do with his decisions. An unfair critic is worse than an unrighteous or ignorant judge, for he deals with creative workmen, the class most sensitive of all to injustice and stupidity. He will be quick to declare what is fine in their work, and will point out errors with the bearing that makes for reform rather than discouragement. On the other hand, he will show no lenience to promoters of flagrant heresy and those whose work is " outlawed of art." Certain of the accused are either highly meritorious or guilty of crime in the first degree. But the maxim *de minimis* also is to be regarded: what is hopelessly dull or insignificant may be left to the gracious law of natural decay.

With respect to fairness and unbiassed judgment, I have observed that sometimes the mere function of critical writing seems, for the time being, to change its exerciser from what he is in his personal life; to make him forget his own tastes, friendships, antipathies; just as in law we have even seen men of unsavory conduct and character, who, when on the bench, are wise and impartial judges. Into the rationale of this I need not go at present. When the best-intentioned person, not fitted by nature and equipment for a judicial calling, usurps it, the exact reverse of this process is apt to be observed.

Criticism itself, after the methods of its eminent professors, often is a constructive art—the promoter of higher standards and creations on the part of those to whom it is addressed. Each of the great critics

[41]

has added a step to the stairway from which it takes a more penetrative and enlarged view. Lessing declared the innate sovereignty of genius. Applying his thought to technics, he discussed the privileges of the respective fine arts and mapped out the border lines across which neither can pass without encroaching on the other's ground. Goethe's generalizations are those of a lofty intellect surveying works of the genius to which it was allied and conscious of the theory of their perfection. Taine, more definitely than others, has regarded environment and heredity as factors, a knowledge of which is wholly indispensable for the consideration of an author's product. Sainte-Beuve's method, so poetic and intuitive, looked into the spiritual growth of the character under notice, always intent upon a subject's personality and seeking in his work the expression of his soul. On similar lines Matthew Arnold probes for the realities of life, thought, action; an Anglo-ethical reverence underlies his judgments, in which a consciousness of the malady disturbing a school, an individual, or a nation, is usually apparent.

I speak of criticism as an art, but there is a science of criticism, as of other arts, and to this fact is due the success of great artists, musicians, poets, architects, etc., in technical comment upon the rules and examples of their respective departments. In this age, whose chief note is a recognition of the " reign of law," it is more than ever fit that these classes should be heard with reference to their own lines of effort, should be Masters in the traditional sense of the appellation. The unformulated instinct of a true artist is scientifically correct. This declares to him that beauty is something absolute and objective—if not an entity, a thing, it at all events lies in *expression*—in the expression and charm of fitness. Only through a course of mental sophistry will he learn to accept the inverted theory of Véron (otherwise the most constructive of modern French critics), who maintains beauty's subjectivity, *i. e.*, its non-existence except as an impression of the observer. Admit Véron's premise, that beauty is a chimera, and you must consider his treatise on "Æsthetics" unimpeachable. It is logical, masterly; but for one I do not think it sound doctrine, and the artistic nature is loath to believe, that " there is no disputing about tastes." I do not admit that Taste— and I use this hackneyed word in its full meaning—is purely the subjective standard of each individual, and that the taste of one is as good as that of another. Beauty everywhere is " a felt conformity to law "—of course to the law of its habitat; hence, again, the expression of the fitness of things, of the Right under the existing conditions. The personal " impressions " of one whose organization does not enable him to perceive that fitness, are no more to us than the visions of the half-blind who " see men as trees walking." And if from a material world or system all sentient observers were to be exiled, certain forms and combinations would still be beautiful in themselves, and would be found so by the first sane intelligence that should arrive to contemplate them.

Taste, therefore, is subjective, because man himself is a microcosm, having the operation of universal

[43]

methods in his own being, and discerning what is in harmony therewith. So far as he discerns this, he has taste; so far as he can utilize it in forming new and ideal structures, he is a creative artist.

The modern effort errs, in its false assumption of freedom, whenever a workman is encouraged to make rules limited to his own capacity. A sane and noble "impressionism" is that which reveals to us the individuality, the distinctive genius of an artist; it is his personal nimbus illuminating his work, but the work must express what is scientifically defensible, or it will be wrong and not enduring. One may wear blue glasses, but that does not make the world blue. Nevertheless, standards of fitness vary, justly, according to varying conditions of region, material, race, etc., beauty being always dependent on these conditions. An edifice like the Parthenon, whose proportions are exquisite, because exactly fitted to their special locality in this special world, would be absurd and unlovely, if not impossible, on another planet. A race inhabiting the latter would find beauty only in a structure subordinated to the conditions of weight, material, color, climate, there existing. Such observers, like the structure, would be part of the distinct local system, and their mental and spiritual nature would not be out of correlation.

Inferior race types have a beauty of their own. This, with its rules and standards, the superior race comprehends and admits for what it is worth. Criticism, therefore, is inclusive. Only a narrow and superficial zealot promulgates restrictive dogmas—such, for instance, as the claim that a striking theme is of no value in art. The general appreciation of an impressive motive or topic, imaginatively presented, and even apart from the technical quality of the work, is something to be recognized by a healthy judgment.

Above all, I conform to the belief that *the great and final office of the critic is to distinguish between what is temporary or modish, and what is enduring, in any phase, type, or product, of human work.* I have said nothing of the humor, sympathy, insight, personal style, which enhance the strength and constitute the charm of critical writing. The foregoing points are merely a restatement of what seems to me the merest primer of criticism, given with as little sophistication as possible and in the briefest space.

III

A BELT OF ASTEROIDS [1]

NOW and then a name becomes durably known in
literature through the reputation of a single
fugitive poem. Our English lyrical system has, of
course, its greater and lesser planets, with their groups
of attendant satellites. At irregular periods, some
comet flashes into view, lights up the skies for a time,
and then disappears beyond the vision. Whether,
after the completion of a cycle, it will again attract
attention and become an accepted portion of this solar
family, or whether, being of a transient though garish
presence, it will lessen forever upon its hyperbolic
skyway, cannot always be determined by observers.
And lastly, at the risk of tearing a metaphor to tatters,
I may say that there are scattered through certain
intervals of the system, like those fragments between
the orbits of Jupiter and Mars, the asteroidal poets,
each of whom we have recognized by a single and
distinctive point of light.

The one effort of an amateur is accepted by the
people, or gains favor with compilers who select and
preserve whatever is of lasting value. The result is
a wide public knowledge of these kinless poems, and

[1] *The Galaxy,* January, 1869.

[46]

of the facts which have attended their begetting; so that I shall not hunt for new matter, or reason too curiously upon my theme. Rather let me associate a few of the best-known and even hackneyed pieces of this sort, while the reader considers the philosophy of their production and success.

One is tempted to borrow a title from the British politicians, who, as everybody knows, called a member of Parliament " Single-Speech Hamilton," after his delivery of a sound and persuasive harangue upon the finances, in November, 1775. If the essence of fun be incongruity, then the nickname was not amiss, for it was certainly incongruous and odd that a member, who had dozed through silent terms, should jump up at a crisis and add unexpected strength to his party by the eloquence of a trained rhetorician and a wisdom which none dreamed he could possess. I have no doubt that, before morning, at the clubs, hundreds and fifties were offered against his ever speaking again. If so, he must have become as obnoxious to those who took the odds as were the portly old buffers who darkened coffee-house windows long beyond the dates at which the younger bucks had wagered that apoplexy would seize them; for Hamilton, having once tasted renown, did, it seems, essay more speeches, thereby putting the nicknamers and gamesters to confusion; which leads De Quincey to remark, with a chuckle over the whimsies of humanity, that the generation " had greatly esteemed the man called Single-Speech Hamilton, not at all for the speech (which, though good, very few people had read), but entirely from

[47]

the supposed fact that he had exhausted himself in one speech, and had been physically incapable of making a second; so that afterward, when he did make a second, everybody was incredulous, until, the thing being demonstrated, naturally the world was disgusted, and most people dropped his acquaintance."

The world is thus jealous of its preconceived opinions, or of rivalry to an established favorite, and will always array the old against the new. It begrudges a chance hand the right to hit the bull's-eye more than once, and measures each successive shot with unkind exactness; so that only those who have the root of the matter in them, and do better and better, are at all advanced by fresh trials after one triumph. A first achievement will be merged, and thought even less of, among equal others of the kind.

That was a shrewder fellow, of our own day and country, who took warning from Hamilton's misfortunes, and delivered *his* single speech at the close of a long Senatorial term, knowing that the loss of an election had put him beyond the perils of anti-climax. Sitting at his desk—he had been a cripple for years—and talking off his speech in the most random manner, he was logical and humorous by turns, drove black care from the Senate Chamber, and threw a singularly grotesque glamor over the last night of that doleful session which preceded the opening of our civil war. Next morning he left in a blaze of glory for Kentucky, and, so far as I know, was never heard of more.

Our business, however, is not with the politicians, but with that superior race, the poets. Not that these songsters are exempted from a common law. If, once in a while, some brown domestic bird varies his wonted piping, and breaks out in passionate and melodious notes; or, when a brilliant-plumed creature, kept rather for ornament than song, seems to have borrowed the throstle's minstrelsy—if these venture again, the one must have lighter trills and quavers, and the other a purer and more assured sweetness, or it will be said of each that

> —he never could recapture
> The first fine careless rapture.

Many a second performance has thus been stifled within the hearing of us all.

He who has discerned and made available the one fortunate moment of his life, has not lived entirely in vain. Multitudes pass through the sacred garden unawares, with their eyes fixed upon illusions far away. Yet there comes to most persons a time when they are lifted above the hard level of common life to the region of spiritual emotion and discovery. The dullest eye will catch glimpses to make one less forlorn; the ear will be suddenly unsealed, and hear the bells of heaven ring; the mouth will be touched with fire, and utter imaginative speech. Were there not something divine in each of us, a poet would find no listeners. Thus the crises of passion, joy and pain, which are inevitable for all, often raise the most plodding to a comprehension of the rapture of the poet, the devotion of the martyr, the assurance of the leader of his kind. The clear vision demands, and for the moment seems to carry with it, a new gift of expression. Men speak with tongues they never knew before; yet, when the Pentecost is over, relapse into their ordinary existence, and wonder no less than others at what it has been given them to do.

A chance lyric composed in this wise, and the sole performance which has interested the world in its author, has frequently seemed to the latter so light a thing that he has neglected to identify his name with its success. Scores of the ballads which mark the growth of our English poetry, and are now gathered and edited as a portion of its history, have given no fame to the minor poets who sang them,

> Ere days that deal in *ana* swarmed
> Their literary leeches.

Doubtless not a few of those notable anonymous pieces, which people love to attribute to some favorite author or hero, have been, could we only determine it, the single productions of amateurs. There is "The Lye," for example, which is claimed for Sir Walter Raleigh, and is quite good enough for him to have written—is better than anything established as his own—yet whose authorship is still in escrow between Raleigh, Sylvester, and others of less repute. There are some plaintive stanzas, which commence, "Defiléd is my name full sore," and profess to be the lament of Queen Anne Boleyne from her prison cell, but are undoubtedly the work of another hand. The

lovers of that soldierly canticle, " How Stands the
Glass Around?" indignant that so lusty and winsome
a child should be a foundling, have tried to fix its
paternity upon Gen. James Wolfe, because that chivalrous Englisher delighted in it, and used to troll it
melodiously across the board. This catch, more
widely recognized by the second stanza—

> Why, soldiers, why
> Should you be melancholy, boys?
> Why, soldiers, why,
> Whose business 'tis to die?

is indeed the perfection of a soldier's banqueting song
—not only pathetic and musical, but with cadences
of rhythm so adjusted that it has a pulsing accent at
intervals which relate to the drum-beat and the martial
tread of ranks. Any poet might be glad to have
composed it. We have it, as copied from a half-sheet
of music printed about the year 1710. Perhaps it
was brought over from the Low Countries by Marl-
borough's men; yet there is the ring of Dryden's
measures about it, and a poet, whose instinct upon
such matters is almost unfailing, has declared to me
that he would venture to ascribe it to glorious John
upon this internal evidence alone. The authors of a
hundred comparatively modern ballads and ditties, like
" The Children in the Wood," " Comin' Thro' the
Rye," " When this old Cap was New," have left
their voices alone behind them; yet each voice seems
to have a distinctive quality of its own. Who wrote
" The White Rose," that darling little conceit of a

Yorkish lover to his Lancastrian mistress? The twin stanzas have become a jewel upon the " stretched fore-finger of all time." James Somerville laid violent hands upon them, early in the last century, remodelled them, and added three verses of his own, each weaker than the predecessor. It has been the fate of many pretty wanderers to be thus kidnapped and rechris-tened, and sometimes, fortunately, by nobler craft than Somerville's, to be changed to something truly rich and rare. As when John Milton based " Il Pen-seroso " upon the verses " In Praise of Melancholy," commencing—

> Hence, all ye vain delights!

and ending

> Here stretch our bones in a still, gloomy valley,
> Nothing's so dainty sweet as lonely melancholy.

These have been claimed for Fletcher, since he inserted them in his play of " The Nice Valour," but possibly were composed by Dr. William Strode, who flourished in the first half of the seventeenth century. Dr. Strode is also thought to have written a lyric often quoted as Dryden's, " The Commendation of Music," which contains some delicate lines:

> Oh, lull me, lull me, charming air,
> My senses rocked with wonder sweet!
> Like snow on wool thy fallings are,
> Soft like a spirit are thy feet.

Campbell found the key-note of his resonant naval ode, "Ye Mariners of England," in the lines, "Ye Gentlemen of England," written by Martyn Parker so long before. Burns worked over the old North Country ballad of "Sir John Barleycorn," as well as many an ancient Scottish song; and Shakespeare— but I need not multiply examples. The rude strong choruses which have sprung up in great campaigns, or at times of revolutionary excitement, have been the offspring of single minds, though verse after verse has been mated with them by the people. Such are the burdens of the French "Malbrouck" and "Ça Ira," the Irish "Shan Van Vocht," and our own grim battle-chorus of "John Brown's Body"—yet it would be difficult to prove that they had not "growed" like Topsy, without the formality of a beginning. I take it, in brief, that many of the noteworthy anonymous poems were the handiwork of single-poem makers. Artists who have become favorably known by continuous effort are not careless of their titles to successful work, nor do the book-wrights often permit specimens of the acknowledged masters to be lost.

The composers of our most familiar random poems are of several types. First, those whose one inspiration has come from a sentiment—like the love of home, of country, of sweetheart, of wife and offspring. Such have sung because a chance emotion would have vent, and their song has found a greeting in the common heart, independently of much artistic right to consideration. Next are the natural rhymesters, with their sound and fury. If one makes verses perpetually, the odds are that he will at some time find something worth to say, or that he will hit upon a theme in which his fellows have a genuine interest; and when these chances come together, the result is a popular acceptation of what is produced, while against the rest of the author's jingles we stop our ears. Again, there are persons of high culture and beautiful thought, who have the gift of expression, but who have neglected its practice, either being sufficient unto themselves, or with their energies so diffused in other walks of life that they have only yielded in a gracious or impassioned moment to utterance of the lays for which we gratefully remember them.

A fugitive poem thus depends for its preservation upon an appeal to the universal emotions; or, through its real merits, gives pleasure to cultured minds, who insure it ultimate renown by Ruskin's process of the transfer of correct taste from the judicious to the unskilful. Here and there one combines these attractions, and thus achieves the high dual purpose of art. A lyric of the first kind often allies itself to an air so taking that we can hardly say whether the poetry or the music has made the hit. But some verses, like " God save the King," are such utter mouthing that their entire success has evidently depended on the tune. If not, old-time British loyalty was a sentiment beyond modern comprehension. Yet there are happy instances in our own language, more frequently among the Scotch and Irish dialects, of " perfect music unto noble words; " while there are other widely popular stanzas, for which musical composers have tried in vain to find a consonant melody, and thus express their very sense.

Among poems which are endeared to the people by their themes is that strictly American production, " The Bucket " of Samuel Woodworth. Without great poetical merit, it calls up simple idyllic memories to every one who has been a country boy, whether he has gained in manhood the prizes of life, or is still a trouble-tossed wanderer. To most Americans, home has been a place to start from, and only loved when left forever. Yet through the sentiment of home and a pleasant sensuous reminiscence of boyhood, " The Bucket " has found its way to numberless hearts. And Woodworth, when writing it, was lifted, for perhaps the only time in his life, to the genuine emotion of the poet, yearning after the sunny meadows, the *fons splendidior vitro,* and the moss-covered bucket of his rustic days. He was indeed a tempest-beaten fellow; a printer, born in Scituate, Mass., and a hard-worked, generally unfortunate hack and journalist, from 1816 down to his death in 1842. Except his one famous song, I can find nothing worth a day's remembrance in his collected poems, of which a volume was published in 1818, and again in 1827. Yet he wrote other pieces in the same metre and with as much care and purpose. His patriotic songs during the war of 1812 had a wide reading, as things went then. All are of the copy-book order; his was a tame, didactic mind; he never wrote but one poem, and that of itself preserves his name. " The Bucket " belongs to the lower or basic strata of the Parnassus mountain—the emotional (yet here it occurs to me that these crop out again near the apex, as in some lofty dramatic outburst, like

Grief fills the room up of my absent child!)

and this household poem, without the factitious aid of a popular air, holds a place by its own music and the associations which it conveys.

Indeed, I am not sure that the present article was not suggested by a visit made one day to the rooms where a painter has translated into his own form of expression this and another of our simplest primary lyrics. Multitudes are now buying the pretty chromolithographs of Jerome Thompson's paintings of "The Old Oaken Bucket," and "Home, Sweet Home"; nor do I hesitate to say that few more grateful and attractive pictures, within the means of the average countrydweller, can hang upon his walls, than these truthful representations of the birth-place of Samuel Woodworth, and the "Sweet Home" of John Howard Payne.[1]

The last-named ditty, though still more obviously depending upon a sentiment, has a world of help from the air to which it was composed. Looking at the

[1] This, without discussion of the merits of the paintings or the good and evil effects of distributing their lithographic copies among the people. It seems to me, however, that Mr. Thompson's pictures have the feeling and suggestiveness of the songs for which they are named; and the colored prints are the most carefully finished of those yet produced in this country.

stirring life and many writings of its author, it seems
strange that such ordinary stanzas should be the production by which he is known, and here mentioned
as his single poem.   Payne was a New Yorker, born
in 1792, and, by an odd coincidence, his first essays
were contributed to a juvenile paper called *The Fly*,
published by Samuel Woodworth at the Boston office,
where the latter learned his trade.   The former was
only seventeen years old when he made a famous sensation at the Park, as Young Norval, following it up
with the enactment of all sorts of parts at many
American theatres, and soon playing as second to
George Frederick Cooke.   He had taken to the stage
for the support of a widowed mother, breaking off a
collegiate course at Union.   In 1813 he went to England and came out at Drury Lane; then turned author
again, and made his first literary success in the tragedy
of " Brutus," which he wrote for Edmund Kean, and
which still holds " the stage."   He also wrote " Virginius " and " Therese," and I don't know what, but
the facts about " Home, Sweet Home " may bear
telling again.   For years Payne was an available playwright and craftsman in the London dramatic world.
When Charles Kemble became manager of Covent
Garden, he purchased a batch of our author's manuscripts for the gross sum of £230; and a play was
fished out from the mess, changed by Payne into an
opera, and produced as " Clari, the Maid of Milan."
Miss Tree, the elder sister of Mrs. Charles Kean, was
in the first cast, and sang " Home, Sweet Home," one
of the " gems " of this piece.   It made an astounding

hit, was speedily the popular favorite, and even at this day we may say that the air and words are the surest key, on the reappearance of a pet *diva,* to unlock the hearts of her welcomers. Those who were present will not forget the return of Kellogg to our Academy on the 19th of last October, and the tenderness and grace with which she sang them; nor the encores of the audience, and the flowers which dropped around her till she seemed like a melodious bird in Eden. "Sweet Home" was only reckoned at £30 to its author, but was a fortune to those who purchased it. In 1832, 100,000 copies had been sold by the original publisher, and the profits within two years after its issue were two thousand guineas. For all this, it is nothing but a homely, unpoetical statement of the most characteristic sentiment of the Teutonic race. The music had gained no former triumph; but wedded to the idea of home, and sounded in Anglo-Saxon ears, it became irresistible, and will hold its own for generations. "'Midst pleasures and palaces" is as bad as bad can be, but match it with the assertion "There's no place like Home!" and we all accept the one for the sake of the other.

Nor is it strange that in America—where homes are so transitory and people are like the brooks which go on forever—this sentiment should take hold as firmly as in the Motherland. It is because our home-tenure here *is* so precarious that we cling to its idealization. Conversely, we have little of that itch to possess land—to own so many roods of earth to the centre —which our adopted citizens display. The Yankee undervalues the attainable, and is so used to see land at low rates about him that he can scarcely understand the eagerness with which a Frenchman or German receives his title-deeds to some barren hillside in Pennsylvania or a quarter section along the overland route.

Payne was too much of an actor to be a poet. His youthful features, judging from the likeness taken in his seventeenth year, were of a singularly mobile and expressive type. Not long ago, some of his MSS., and a portrait of him in later manhood, were offered for sale in this city, as a part of a virtuoso's collection. The face there given would readily have obtained a place in Eugene Benson's gallery of those which are beautiful and suggestive. He was, also, too much of a playwright and author to become a great actor; and too much a man of affairs to stick to any profession continuously. As last he made a long retirement, as Consul at Tunis, and might have produced an epic if he had known how. Before this, his employments were as diverse as those of Shakespeare; but the gap between the capacities of two such beings is wide as the arch from pole to pole, though they stand on a common axis of chosen work.

As for Payne's one song, it would seem that any stanzas, thus widely known and endeared, have a more than ordinary claim for admission to a collection which aims to present the noteworthy accepted poetry of the English language. So that, while glad to repeat the general approval of Mr. Dana's volume, and to acknowledge that it contains, on the whole, the most conscientious, scholarly, and catholic presentation which has yet been made—I am surprised that the critical editor has not, in the case of " Home, Sweet Home," so far overstepped his limit of the " truly beautiful and admirable " as to admit it. Of course it goes to the rear on the score of poetical defects; but on what ground are introduced the more objectionable stanzas of " God Save the King "? As the national British anthem? But " Home, Sweet Home " is the people's and children's song of all English-speaking countries, and its very title is a plea for a humble corner in any Household Book of Poetry.

Mention of " God Save the King " suggests national hymns, and we notice that the leading patriotic songs of France, England, and the United States, are the single works of their authors, unless we allow George Saville Carey's claim that his father wrote the British national anthem, and give credit to Queen Hortense for the words as well as the pretty music of " Partant pour la Syrie." For Hortense, with all her faults, was a sweet musician and verse-maker, and executed other agreeable works; yet in her best-known song most exactly expressed the courtly, chivalrous vivacity of a people who fight and make love *pari passu,* and gaily interblend their patriotism, gallantry, and love of fame. Both the poem and the music have that " quality " which, refined by culture, so wins us in the minor art of France. Despite their " temporary and trivial " nature they have other claims to the affection of her people than the accident of the Second

Empire. After all, they are not quite the thing, and the French Minister of War is advertising for a worthy national hymn. He will scarcely obtain it from a leading poet. Mr. Grant White has told us how national hymns are written and not written, and it is a fact that nearly all which have not grown among the people, have resulted from the glow of patriotism in the hearts of citizen-laymen, with whom love of country was a compelling inspiration.

The " Marseillaise " is a preëminent example of a single lyrical outburst from the soul of an unprofessional poet. It is the real battle-hymn of an oppressed France, and in her struggles for liberty will never be supplanted by any manufactured successor. After a long suppression, it was again made the national song when Louis Philippe gained the throne by the revolution of 1830; but when the Citizen-King forgot his citizenship, he, too, was compelled to flee before its chorus. It is the most historical and dramatic of lyrics. The one flight which Rouget-de-Lisle took was that of an eagle, soaring to the empyrean, and disdaining a lower reach. When a soldier invades the province of the poet, composes such a song at a single heat, and, like the bards of old, summons from his harp the music that shall match them, it is not safe to deny anything to the inspiration of mere amateurs. The man's whole life was crowded into that night at Strasbourg, and with it all the frenzy and devotion of a bleeding land.

Both our American national poems are the compositions of lawyers, who are known for little else which they wrote, outside the judicial reports. Neither seems to have had any sacred fury in his nature that was not evoked by patriotism. That which Judge Joseph Hopkinson gave out in " Hail, Columbia," was of a sufficiently humdrum kind. He had the music of the " President's March " as a copy before him, and his verses are little better or worse than the air. The Judge was born in 1770, and was a spruce young lawyer in the summer of 1798, when war with France seemed imminent, and Congress was holding an excited session at Philadelphia. He wrote his ode at a sitting, for the benefit of an actor, who had vainly exhausted the poets of the theatrical company, in an effort to adopt words to the stilted march then most in favor. Hopkinson was appealed to on Saturday, wrote the song on Sunday, heard it from a stage-box on the next evening; and it made a great sensation. The citizens joined in the chorus night after night, and the jurist-author found himself renowned for life by a rude homily upon Columbia in prose chopped to the metre. He was afterward a member of Congress, then a Judge of the United States District Court, and died within the memory of most of us at the good old age of seventy-two.

Francis Scott Key swept the chords more tunefully in his " Star-Spangled Banner," which has merits that would give it a leasehold, independently of the spirited music to which it was composed. Its obvious rhymes and adjectives—" haughty host," " dread silence," " foul footsteps' pollution," etc., are little suited to the naturalism of our later day, but the burden,

'Tis the star-spangled banner; O long may it wave
O'er the land of the free and the home of the brave!

was that which a popular refrain should be, the strong
common sentiment of a nation; and Key, for once in
his life, expressed the feeling of a true poet.   He died
shortly after Hopkinson, whose junior he was by seven
years.   He wrote some religious pieces, and a few
other songs, none of which have outlived their period;
though one, " On the Return of Decatur," had a brief
reputation.   It is in the Adams-and-Liberty metre of
the " Star-Spangled Banner," and exemplifies the sing-
song rhythm into which men like Woodworth and Key
are apt to fall, and which often commends itself to
the popular taste.   It is the bacon-and-greens, so to
speak, of the feast of song, and not much relished by
cultivated palates.

That most original and resonant lyric, the " Carmen
Bellicosum " of Guy Humphrey McMaster, is far removed from these, except by the common theme of defence of country.   Here is a noble chant indeed!
Trumbull, in his pictures, effected no more than this
writer has given us with a single dash of the pen—an
interpretation of the very spirit of '76.   The " Carmen
Bellicosum "—every one will recall its opening verse,

In their ragged regimentals
Stood the old Continentals,
Yielding not.

occupies a unique position among English lyrics.
There is nothing like it in our language; 'tis the ring-

ing, characteristic utterance of an original man. There is a perfect wedding of sense to sound, and of both to the spirit of the theme. To include a picture often ruins a song; but here we have the knot of patriots clustered upon a battle-hillside, the powder cracking amain, the old-fashioned colonel galloping with drawn sword, and as

> Rounder, rounder, rounder, roars the old six-pounder,
>   Hurling death,

it seems a heavier piece of ordnance, and charged with weightier issues, than the whole park of artillery in a modern armament.

The song will last with the memory of revolutionary days. I know little of its author, save that he is also a lawyer and a judge, presiding over the Steuben County Court in this, his native State. He is now about forty years of age, and must have been quite young when his " Carmen " appeared in the old *Knickerbocker Magazine*. If a stripling attorney will enter the minstrel lists, sound such a potent blast, then withdraw himself to the happy life of a country-gentleman, nor be heard again through all these years, he also must, for the present, be numbered in our catalogue of the single-poem poets.

McMaster is a Scotch or North-Irish patronymic, and the Scotch have ever been in the custom of producing fugitive lyrics of a true poetical quality. These ditties relate more frequently to the strongest of all emotions—that of love between man and woman—

than to the love of home or fatherland. Two of the sweetest will at once recur to the reader. "Auld Robin Gray" was composed by Anne Lyndsay, afterward Lady Barnard, as long ago as 1772, at Balcarras in Fife. Her father was the Earl of that ilk. She was an elegant, spirited girl, not yet out of her teens, when an old air, set to a loose old song, "The Bridegroom grat when the sun gaed doun," gave her a motive for her work. The lassie had learned the tune, in such mischievous ways as our liberal maids doubtless know of in these prudish times, and thought the pensive measure deserved more fitting words. She chose for her text the world-wide plaint that "Crabbed Age and Youth cannot live together"—a theme as ancient in English as Chaucer's "January and May" —took the name of Gray from an old herd in the vicinage, and wrote as sweet and pathetic a ballad as exists in any tongue. The first stanza,

When the sheep are in the fauld and the kye at hame.

is now, I believe, the only one sung to the antique tune. From the second, "Young Jamie lov'd me weel," to the close, the music, written thirty years since by the Rev. W. Lewes, is still most in use. Lady Anne's ballad was not given to the public till 1776, and, as it at once became famous, a prolonged dispute arose concerning its authorship. Modesty prevented the authoress from claiming her laurels. How could a debonair young maiden own herself familiar with the wanton ditty, "The Bridegroom grat"? Not till she had been many years the wedded wife of Sir Andrew Barnard, and the shadows of death were close at hand, did she write her letter to Sir Walter, avowing the authorship, and narrating at length what I have briefly told. She composed a few other verses, but nothing to compare with the ballad for which we remember her name.

There is pretty good warrant for saying that the soldiers' darling, " Annie Laurie," was the work of Mr. Douglas, of Fingland, who courted Anne, a fair daughter of Sir Robert Laurie, the first baronet of Maxwelton. This was near the commencement of the last century. The song, as it now exists, is generally classed as anonymous in our anthologies; but has been so refined and annealed through various crucibles that the current version is quite different from the two stanzas which Douglas wrote, and certainly more artistic. His are thus given in the *Ballad Book,* which contains the earliest printed copy:

> Maxwelton banks are bonnie
>   Where early fa's the dew;
> Where I and Annie Laurie
>   Made up the promise true;
> Made up the promise true,
>   And never forget will I,
> And for bonnie Annie Laurie
>   I'd lay me doun and die.
>
> She's backit like a peacock,
>   She's breistit like a swan,
> She's jimp about the middle,
>   Her waist you weel micht span;

[66]

A BELT OF ASTEROIDS

> Her waist you weel micht span;
>   And she has a rolling eye,
> And for bonnie Annie Laurie
>   I'd lay me doun and die.

The heroine's rolling eye cast its glances away from poor Douglas, and she married a Mr. Ferguson, of Craigdarrock, who found some better mode of winning a maiden's heart than singing under her windowpanes. After all, the pleasure is as great in loving as in being loved; and, to put the matter allegorically, Apollo, indignant at the slight inflicted by Venus upon his servant, gave him, unawares, a seat in his temple, and ordained that, for centuries, lovers should sing the song of him who sang in vain.

What manlier love-poetry was ever written than the verses, "To his Mistress," of James Grahame, Marquis of Montrose, wherein he vowed

> I'll make thee famous by my pen,
>   And glorious by my sword!

The poem itself fulfilled half the pledge. More than two hundred years have gone by, and still no lines are more often quoted than this quatrain from the same lyric:

> He either fears his fate too much,
>   Or his deserts are small,
> Who dares not put it to the touch
>   To gain or lose it all.

Not more famous is the distich,

> Stone walls do not a prison make,
> Nor iron bars a cage,

from Dick Lovelace's stanzas " To Althæa, from Prison"; though the handsome cavalier left many another ditty to distinguish him from our birds of a single flight.   The lines here mentioned are the second example we have reached of the music, real or imagined, of imprisoned songsters; and to them I might add the Latin verses, *" In Dura Catena,"* attributed to the Queen of Scots—certainly the one poem written by the Fayre Gospeller, Anne Askewe, who was burned at the stake by command of brutal and dying Harry, in 1546.   After her last examination upon the rack, she was inspired to utter, in a Newgate cell, the heroic defiance :

> Like as the arméd knight
>   Appointed to the field,
> With this world will I fight,
>   And faith shall be my shield.

We can well believe the statement of one who saw the girl led to execution, that " she had an angel's countenance and a smiling face."   Poor Anne's verses have been preserved rather for her story's sake and for their religious ardor, than for poetical excellence; and it is noticeable that hymns, and fugitive lyrics animated with religious hope or aspiration, have a fairer chance, other things being equal, of obtaining a continued hearing than almost any class—those appealing to the "master passion" alone excepted. Reflective poems, tinged with that melancholy which comes to one chastened by the experiences of life, are also widely in favor.

"I would not live Alway" has everywhere made the name of our venerable citizen, Dr. Muhlenberg, a household word. He wrote it many years since, with no thought that it would ever be used for the devotions of the church, but has long seen it in the hymnology of most Protestant denominations, and encountered many pseudo-claimants to its authorship. Among these I knew an old printer, of Litchfield, Connecticut, who imagined he had composed it, and periodically filled a column in the village newspaper with evidence to further his claim. But Dr. Muhlenberg's title cannot be shaken. Another poem, upon a kindred theme, though with the element of hope omitted, was popular with the sad Calvinists of the last generation, but had almost faded out, when an accidental connection with the name of President Lincoln gave it a new lease of life, which may continue with the memory of the great Liberator. He was so fond of repeating the monody,

O why should the spirit of mortal be proud?

that by some persons he was credited with its composition, until the press recognized the work of William Knox, who died A. D. 1825, at Edirburgh, in his thirty-seventh year. These lines are expressive of a brooding Scotch melancholy, pitched in a minor religious key, and in certain moods not ineffective as a quaint and forceful meditation upon an ever-pressing theme. Their whole motive is condensed in the terse old formula, " All flesh is grass "; but a Sicilian poet, the pagan Moschus, found even this an insufficient image of the hopelessness of mortality. Let me give a naked translation (from the wonderful Epitaph of Bion), of the most sorrowful passage ever constructed outside of Hebrew writ:

Even the mallows—alas! alas!—when once in the garden
They, or the pale-green parsley and crisp-growing anise, have perished,
Afterward they will live and flourish again at their season;

We, the great and brave, or the wise—when death has benumbed us—
Deaf in the hollow ground a silent, infinite slumber
Sleep; forever we lie in the trance that knoweth no waking.

The drear and homely verses of Mr. Lincoln's favorite poem have already gained the suffrage of those gentlemen whose favor is such an omen of longevity— the makers of school-books. I find it in the latest *Reader,* along with such selections as Lincoln's " Address at Gettysburg," Read's " Sheridan's Ride," Bayard Taylor's " Scott and the Veteran," Whittier's " Barbara Freitchie," and other new-born pieces, which are to the rising generation what the " Speech of Patrick Henry," " Marco Bozzaris," or " Stand! the Ground's Your Own, My Braves!" were to ourselves, a few—it seems a *very* few—summers and winters ago.

Sexagenarians can remember the notoriety given Herbert Knowles—an English youth who died at Canterbury in his twentieth year—by Robert Southey, who set him forth in the *London Quarterly* as a second Kirke White. Knowles was a precocious religious poet, and his surviving verses are " Lines Written in the Churchyard of Richmond," to the text, Matt. xvii., 4:

> Methinks it is good to be here!
> If thou wilt, let us build, but to whom?

These will appear in many future compilations; and so will the thoughtful numbers of our own countrywoman, Harriet Winslow:

> Why thus longing, thus forever sighing
> For the far-off, unattained and dim?

But a more impassioned and elevated single poem is that fervent composition imagined to have been written by " Milton on his Blindness "—the work of a Quaker lady, Elizabeth Lloyd,[1] of Philadelphia. These truly " noble numbers " deserve the attention which they gained upon their first appearance, at which time paragraphists went so far as to call them Milton's own, and credit them to an Oxford edition of his poems. They are not Miltonic in the least, but exhibit a rapturous inspiration, and of themselves have insured their writer a long regard.

[1] Now Mrs. E. L. Howell.

Occasionally straightforward rhymes, with a moral, like " The Three Warnings " of Mrs. Hester Lynch Piozzi—Johnson's Mrs. Thrale—have held their own, either for their shrewd wisdom, or for the associations connected with their author.

But which of all the asteroids that have passed before our vision—whether tinged with a domestic, patriotic, amorous, or sombre light—will be longer or more lovingly regarded than the children's own poem and dearest—" 'Twas the Night before Christmas "? written for them so daintily by a sage college professor, Clement C. Moore, to wit, long time a resident of this old Dutch city, and deceased (peace to his ashes!) hardly more than four or five years ago. " A Visit from St. Nicholas " is dear to the little ones for its exquisite fancies and the annual legend, and to us all for our beautiful memories of childhood and home. It is linked with the natal festival of Christendom, is entirely true to its purpose, and finished as deftly as if the author had been a professional poet. Few of those who were his contemporaries, and who know every word of this sparkling fantasia, have been familiar with the details of his quiet and industrious life. He was born in 1779, and grew up a studious philologist, as his Hebrew and English lexicon, issued in 1809, still attests. Twelve years afterward he was made Professor of Biblical Learning in the New York Episcopal Theological Seminary, and more lately took the chair of Oriental and Greek Literature. Despite all this, and rich besides, he wrote poetry, and a volume of his rhymes appeared in 1844. They were of an ephemeral nature, except the poem which I would have gone far to hear him repeat in his old, old age, and for which my younger readers must always remember his venerable name.

Let us not overlook a lyric, of which many have, probably, already thought—the Rev. Charles Wolfe's "Burial of Sir John Moore." No fugitive piece has had a wider or more potential circulation than this school-boy favorite; yet who, besides the men of letters, have troubled themselves concerning its author, or known of other graceful verses by his hand? A few have read the song which he made to the Irish air, "Grammachree." It is said that he sang the music over until it affected him to tears, and impelled him to write his equally pathetic lament, in such stanzas as the following:

> If I had thought thou couldst have died
>   I might not weep for thee;
> But I forgot when by thy side,
>   That thou couldst mortal be.
> It never through my mind had past
>   The time would e'er be o'er,[1]
> And I on thee should look my last,
>   And thou shouldst smile no more!

But we must here cease our observation of poets who come strictly within the prescribed limits of the telescopic field. I have barely space enough for refer-

---

[1] The blemish in this line would not be overlooked by a poet of Wolfe's quality, in these days of mosaic art.

ence to a few of those whose reputation has been won
by life-long devotion to their art, yet of whose respective productions some one piece has, in each instance, gained the world's ear, and often to the neglect
of other excellent works. The poems hitherto considered are more widely known than their authors;
while to name a poet of the class to which I now
allude, is to start in the mind the key-measure of his
representative poem. Examples of this effect are always numerous, and especially in present remembrance
of the poets who wrote long ago—Time so winnows
out and sets apart the general choice, whether it be
such coarse healthful grain as that from which jovial
Bishop Still brewed his " Good Ale "—

> Back and side go bare, go bare;
>   Both foot and hand go cold;
> But belly, God send thee good ale enough,
>   Whether it be new or old!

or the golden barley on which singing birds like
Thomas Lodge and Sir Henry Wotton had fed, ere
they warbled such dainty lyrics as " Love in my bosom
like a Bee," and " You meaner beauties of the night."
These two, and many another canticle of their period,
you can find in R. H. Stoddard's most choice selection of English *Melodies and Madrigals*. Are James
Shirley and Edmund Waller popularly remembered
by single lyrics? Nearly so, for in the one case the
two stanzas of Shirley's " Victorious Men of Earth,"
with the alteration of a couplet, would be in the stately

measures of that grandest and most solemn of our minor poesies, " Death's Final Conquest,"

> The glories of our birth and state
> Are shadows, not substantial things.

while the feeling and theme of the two lyrics are alike, and, though each is perfect in itself, they read like portions of a divided poem. And Waller's name is still popularly connected with " Go, Lovely Rose," and " On a Girdle," out of the whole mass of his songs, epistles, epitaphs, and panegyrics, though Professor Lowell, in his delightful citation of Dryden, and perhaps animated by that scorn of Waller's truckling which every true and noble poet must feel, says that the latter has lived mainly on the credit of a single couplet in the lines closing his " Divine Poesy."

The late English period, however, is all that I can glance at. To mention John Logan is to revive the " Ode to the Cuckoo," yet 'tis by no means certain that Logan did not refine this standard poem from the crude metal left by his friend Michael Bruce. His song on a wild old theme, touched by so many melodists, " The dowie dens of Yarrow," deserves as long a reputation; though of all the Yarrow ballads, that by William Hamilton, " Busk ye, busk ye, my bonnie, bonnie bride! " is the nonpareil. Every one has been affected by the simplicity, music, and exquisite pathos of Caroline Oliphant, the Baroness Nairn's " Land o' the Leal ":

I'm wearin' awa', John,
Like snow-wreaths in thaw, John;
I'm wearin' awa'
      To the land o' the leal.

The author died in 1845, at the ripe age of eighty
years, and throughout her life wrote poetry, some of
it humorous, which was quite the fashion in Scotland.
" The Laird o' Cockpen " had a wide reading, and is
excellent of its kind.   There was Susanna Blamire,
the " Muse of Cumberland," who made sweet use of
the border dialect in her ballads and songs.   " The
Siller Crown " is always associated with her name :

      And ye sall walk in silk attire,
         And siller hae to spare,
      Gin ye'll consent to be his bride
         Nor think o' Donald mair.

There, also, is Sheridan's granddaughter, Lady Duf-
ferin, who has composed very many lyrics, but is
known by her most beautiful ballad, " The Irish Emi-
grant's Lament," sometimes wrongly credited to her
sister, Mrs. Norton.   The words of " I'm Sitting on
the Stile, Mary!" and the genuine melody to which
they are sung, have that about them which will last.
Did Dennis Florence M'Carthy or John Francis Waller write " Dance light, for my heart lies under your
feet, love "?   I should like to know, for equal authorities ascribe it to one and the other, and it is too graceful an Irish ballad to go a-begging; 'tis almost as good
as the song of Irish songs, Allingham's " Lovely Mary

Donnelly." Of Thomas Noel's *Rhymes and Roundelays,* published in London, 1841, the poem all know is a strange and grotesque lyric, "The Pauper's Drive," with its dreary burden:

> Rattle his bones over the stones!
> He's only a pauper, whom nobody owns.

Perhaps "Give me the Old," written by R. H. Messenger, a Bostonian, from the theme "Old Wine to Drink," etc., should have been included with the class first under review. The New Yorker, James Aldrich, made verses innumerable, but we only speak of two little stanzas, entitled "A Death Bed," so curiously like and unlike Hood's "We watched her breathing through the Night." The names of three poets—and on whom in the South have fallen their mantles?—quickly bring to mind three songs which won them most lovers; remembering the scholar, poet, and enthusiast, Richard Henry Wilde, one finds himself murmuring that soft perfection, "My Life is like the summer Rose"; next comes Edward C. Pinkney's chivalrous "Health"; "I drink this cup to one made up of loveliness alone!" and with mention of Philip Pendleton Cooke, all think of "Florence Vane," which, however, is a close study after E. A. Poe. The latter is himself constantly entitled the author of "The Raven," yet, for true poetical qualities, his "Annabel Lee," "Haunted Palace," "The City in the Sea," and that remarkable dithyrambic fantasy, "The Bells," are more valued by the selectest taste. Why does every one speak of the late General Morris as the writer of " Woodman, Spare that Tree "? Because this lyric, almost as widely known as " Sweet Home," has the simple elements of a song proper, and in this respect might not have been so good if the author had been a greater poet. I think it deserves a corner, opposite the other, in any liberal collection of our songs. Hoffman's " Sparkling and Bright " had a like trick of catching the public ear. The Rev. Ralph Hoyt, who once published a volume of quaint and original poems, is known as the author of " Old," and he has been so long silent that it is not wholly my fault if he is not reckoned with the list of contemporaries. Two fugitive lyrics, now in my mind, may belong rather to the classification first made, though why I should here select them, I can hardly tell. One is " The Voice of the Grass,"

Here I come creeping, creeping everywhere!

by Sarah Roberts, of New Hampshire. The other—who is it by?—" In Summer when the days were long." Each was composed by a true poet, and is an addition to literature in its unpretending way.

But to return for a moment to our main purpose. The fortunate single-poems, before mentioned, were either the spirited efforts of amateurs, or the sole hits achieved by the Quinces and Triplets of their day. If a person of culture has made, with easy hand, a chance success; or, if patient dullards woo our gracious Thea until they flatter her into a smile of favor, or

[78]

steal upon an unguarded moment to catch certain echoes of her voice; all this is nothing in behalf of amateur art—nor are they to be placed on a level with the consecrated poets. For the latter can, with certainty, again and again, excel the random work of those who come not in by the appointed door. A large proportion of the minor art of our most approved poets is made up of pieces, each of which, if the only specimen of its author, might have received preservation as an attractive fugitive poem. We need not mention the great names of the past, but can any doubt that such would be the case with Browning's " Evelyn Hope," and " How they brought the good news from Ghent to Aix"; with Tennyson's " May Queen," " Bugle Song," " Come into the Garden, Maud"; with Longfellow's " Excelsior"; Lowell's " The Courtin'," and " To a Dandelion"; Bryant's " The Battle-Field"; with those exquisite quatrains by Aldrich, " Ah, sad are they who know not love!" with Boker's " Dirge for Phil Kearny," Winter's beautiful lyric, " Love's Queen," Taylor's " Bedouin Song," and " Daughter of Egypt"; with Swinburne's " If love were what the rose is"; or, indeed, with scores of other imaginative and finished specimens of these and other master-hands? For I have mentioned the foregoing at merest hap-hazard, as minor productions likely, from one cause or another, to have become endeared to the people or the critical few, and each for itself to have preserved an author's name.

Hereafter, more than ever, there will be no royal

road to the honors of the poet. It is necessary, in this period, that every cabinet picture or sketch should show the hand of the master, and be a gem of its kind. More is required to make good work distinctive. High technical finish is so well understood, that it is again asked of the poet, not only that he shall have the art of sweet-saying, but that he shall have something to say. Mrs. Browning sings of the great Pan, down among the river reeds, " making a poet out of a man "; but often I wish some power would make *men* out of plenty of the modern poets. A painter has to look through the Old World for his masterpieces, and to sit long at the feet of his elders for the secrets of color and form; but the versifier's greatest models are at hand in every village library, and the contagion which the press brings to our doors constantly leads hundreds to mistake inclination for power, or an imitative knowledge of the *technique* of poetry for a true inspiration. They catch the knack of making such verses as only genius could have invented fifty years ago, and which then might justly have won them laurels.

Thus no art is so easy as that of poetry; but in none is it so difficult to achieve a distinctive individuality. It is the lowest and highest of arts. In it, more than in any other, amateur work is to be discouraged, as most easily essayed, and as fostering dilettanteism and corrupt taste. There is little danger of sending away angels unawares. I was in the studio of a wise and famous painter, who has learned the secrets of the dawn, when a young aspirant came with a specimen of his work, and sought counsel as to his adoption of the painter's art as a calling for life. My friend looked at the sketch, kindly talked with the youth of a painter's struggles and self-denials, and of the tide constantly pressing the finest genius back from its goal, and so sent his listener away with few words of encouragement or hope. " Now," said I, " you know that boy's picture had merit; why did you treat him so harshly?" He answered, " If he has the right stuff in him, this will make no difference; he will paint on, though the ghost of Raphael should warn him to give way; and will succeed in his art. If he has not, I am doing him the highest benefit by keeping from him that ' crown of sorrow ' which is inevitable for one who has not clearly discerned the true purpose of his life." [1]

[1] Reference may be appreciated by some readers of this essay to *Famous Single and Fugitive Poems*, edited by Rossiter Johnson, published, 1880, by Messrs. Henry Holt & Co., New York.—THE EDITORS.

IV

KEATS [1]

O N the slope of a " peak in Darien," in the shadow
of the very ridge where stood the Spaniard,

> . . . when with eagle eyes
> He stared at the Pacific, and all his men
> Looked at each other with a wild surmise,

my fellow-traveller captured a superb blue moth, of a
species so rare and so difficult to secure that the natives
sell one at the price of a day's labor. We took the
beautiful creature with us on our transit, and deli-
cately leashed it that night to the jalousies of our
veranda on the plaza of the city of Panama. There,
far within the old town, a mate was fluttering around
it at sunrise,—to me a miracle, yet one predicted by
my friend the naturalist. It is just as safe to predict
that young poets will chance upon one another, among
millions; " there's a special providence " in their conjunction and forgathering, instinct and circumstance
join hands to bring this about. The name of Keats
is set within a circlet of other names,—those of Clarke,
Reynolds, Hunt, Charles Brown, the artists Haydon

[1] *The Century Magazine,* February, 1884.

and Severn,—each of which is brighter for the fact that its owner gave something of his love and help to the poet whose name outshines them all. The name itself, at first derided as uncouth, has become a portion of the loveliness which once he made more lovely; it belongs to an ideal now so consecrate that all who watched with him, if but for an hour, have some part of our affections. Among these, if last not least, Severn, who shut out his own fair prospects, relieved a comrade's agony and want, accompanied him along the edge of a river that each must cross alone, until, as sings the idyllist, the eddy seized him, and Daphnis went the way of the stream.

Cowden Clarke, Keats's earliest companion in letters, son of his head-master at the Enfield school, first put Spenser into his hands. At the vital moment, when the young poet had begun to plume his wings, Clarke also made him known to Leigh Hunt, of all men in England the one it behooved him to meet. Hunt, whose charming taste was almost genius, had become—and largely through his influence upon associates—the promoter of a renaissance; he went to the Italian treasure-house, where Chaucer and Shakespeare had been before him, and also, like them, disdained not our natural English tongue and the delight of English landscape—the greenest idyl upon earth. In many ways, since fortunate guidance will save even genius years of groping, he shortened the course by which Keats found the one thing needful, the key to his proper song. When the youth settled down for a real effort, he went off by himself, as we know,

wrote "Endymion," and outdid his monitor in lush
and swooning verse. But it was always Hunt who
unerringly praised the finest, the most original phrases
of one greater than himself, and took joy in assuring
him of his birthright.

Shelley, too, Keats met at this time,—the peer who
was to sing his dirge and pæan. Meanwhile, his own
heroic instinct, the prescience of a muse "that with
no middle flight intends to soar," was shown by his
recognition of the greatest masters as he found them,
—Chaucer, Spenser, Chapman, Shakespeare, Milton,
—and his serious study of few besides. One must
have exemplars and preceptors; let these be of the
best. Neophytes often are drawn to the imitators of
imitators, the catch-penny favorites of the hour, and
this to their own belittlement. The blind still lead
the blind. Give an aspirant the range of English song,
see the masters that attract him, and it is not hard
to cast his horoscope.

Pity is akin to love, when not too self-conscious of
good fortune and the wisdom that leads thereto.
Keats died so young, and so piteously, that some
writers, to whom his work has yielded profit and
delight, naïvely regard him from the superior person's
critical or moral point of view. Lowell, however,
pays honor to the "strong sense" underlying his sensibility. When Mr. Lowell said that "the faults of
Keats's poetry are obvious enough," he plainly had
in mind the faults of the youth's early work,—ex-
travagances from which he freed himself by covering
them in that sculptured monument, "Endymion," with

divine garlands and countless things of worth that beguile us once and again to revisit their tomb. Nor can we take him to task for careless rhymes thrown off in his correspondence. Of their kind, what juvenile letters are better, and who would not like to receive the letters of such a poet at play? Keats is the one metrical artist, in his finer productions, quite without fault, wearing by right, not courtesy, the epithet of Andrea del Sarto. Rich and various as are the masterpieces of the language, I make bold to name one of our shorter English lyrics that still seems to me, as it seemed to me ten years ago, the nearest to perfection, the one I would surrender last of all. What should this be save the " Ode to a Nightingale," so faultless in its varied unity and in the cardinal qualities of language, melody, and tone? A strain that has a dying fall; music wedded to ethereal passion, to the yearning that floods all nature, while

> . . . more than ever seems it rich to die,
> To cease upon the midnight with no pain.

Then what pictures, echoes, immortal imagery and phrase! Can a word or passage be changed without an injury, and by whom? The " Ode on a Grecian Urn " is a more objective poem, moulded like the cold Pastoral it celebrates, radiant with the antique light and joy. Could Beauty speak, even thus might she declare herself. We term Keats a Grecian, and assuredly the English lad created, in latest-born and loveliest semblance, the entire breed of " Olympus' faded hierarchy." But what of " The Eve of St.

Agnes"? Is it not the purest mediæval structure in our verse—a romance-poem more faultless, in the strict sense of the word, than larger models of earlier or later date? In proportion, color, exquisite detail, it is comparable to some Gothic hall or chapel of the best period; and just as surely "Isabella" is Florentine, and equally without flaw. These poems are none the less charged with high imaginings, Keats being one of the few whose imagination is not lessened by technical supremacy. The sonnet on Chapman's Homer was, in this respect, a foretaste of the large utterance to which he afterward attained. "Hyperion," with its Titanic opening and Doric grandeur of tone inviolate from first to last, was a work which the author, with half his power still in reserve, left unfinished, in the loftiest spirit of self-criticism, avowing that it had too many Miltonic inversions. The word "faults" is, in truth, the last to use concerning Keats. His limitation was one of horizon, not of blemish within its bounds.

As regards verbal expression, a close test of original power, he certainly outranks any poet since Shakespeare. Others are poets and something more, or less, —reformers, men of the world, or, like Körner and Chénier, aglow for heroic action. Keats had but one ambition; he was all poet, and I think he would have remained so. However possible the grotesque changes contrived for Byron and Burns in Hawthorne's fantastic draft of "P's Correspondence," the romancer felt that Keats would never become transformed, and pictured him as still true to the ideal. Shelley wor-

shipped Goodness and Truth in the Beauty to which
he vowed that he would dedicate his powers. Of
Keats, one may say that his genius was Beauty's other
self. In " Wuthering Heights," Catharine Earnshaw
avows: " I *am* Heathcliff! He's always, always in
my mind: not as a pleasure, any more than I am always a pleasure to myself, but as my own being."
And Keats *was* Beauty, with the affinity and passion
of soul for soul.

It is hard to hold him to account for an early death
from inherited tendency to phthisis, aggravated by
bleeding at the hands of an old-time surgeon, or for
the publication, after sixty years, of his turbid love-
letters to Fanny Brawne,—letters in which, though
probably the recipient flattered herself otherwise, there
is less of the real Keats than in the most trivial verse
he ever wrote. If you would know an artist's true
self, you must discover it through his art. It was
deplorable that these poor letters should be brought to
light; let us at least give them no more than their true
proportion in our measure of the writer's strength and
weakness. Mr. Arnold is warranted in contempt for
those who enjoy the one letter that he quotes, and who
profess to consider it a " beautiful and characteristic
production." It reveals, as he asserts, " complete en-
ervation," and I own that for the moment Keats
appears to be " passion's slave." Nevertheless, why
yield one jot or tittle to the implication that the old
taunt of Blackwood's is sustained by this letter of a
" surgeon's apprentice,"—that anything " under-bred
and ignoble " can be postulated from even the entire

series of these spasmodic epistles? A theory that such a youth as Keats was " ill brought up " cannot be thus deduced; the reverse, all things considered, seems to have been the case. Furthermore, it may be that the evolution of a poet advances quite as surely through experience of the average man's folly and emotion as through a class training in reticence, dignity, and self-restraint. In the first glow of ambition Keats inscribed "Endymion" to the memory of Chatterton, and gladly would have equalled that sleepless soul in fate, so were he equal to him in renown. Afterward, in his first experience of passion, he yielded to morbid sentiment, self-abandonment, the frenzy of a passing hour. It is not out of nature that genius, in these early crises, should be pitifully sensitive or take stage-strides. The training that would forestall this might, like Aylmer's process, too well remove a birth-mark. We can spare, now and then, a gray head on green shoulders, if thereby we gain a poet. Keats was a sturdy, gallant boy at school,—as a man, free from vices patrician or plebeian, and a gentleman in motive and bearing. No unusual precocity of *character* goes with the artistic temperament. It is observed of born musicians, who in childhood have mastered instrument and counterpoint, and of other phenomenal geniuses, that they are not old beyond their years, nor less simple and frolicsome than their playmates. But the heyday in the blood has always been as critical to poets as the " sinister conjunction " was to the youth of the Arabian tale. Shakespeare, Milton, Burns, Shelley, Byron, were not specifically apostles of common sense in their love-affairs, but their own experience scarcely lowered the tone or weakened the vigor of their poetry. Keats's ideality was disturbed by the passion which came upon him suddenly and late; he clung to its object with fiercer longing and anguish as he felt both her and life itself slipping away from his hold. Everything is extreme in the emotion of a poet. Mr. Arnold does justice to his probity and for-bearance, to his trust in the canons of art and rigid self-measurement by an exacting standard; he surely must see, on reflection, that such a man's slavery to passion would be a short-lived episode. Before Keats could rise again to higher things, his doom confronted him. His spirit flew hither and thither, by many paths: across each, as in Tourguéneff's prose-poem, yawned the open grave, and behind him the witch Fate pressed ever more closely. He had prayed " for ten years " in which he might overwhelm himself in poesy. He was granted a scant five, and made transcendent use of them. Had he lived, who can doubt that he would have become mature in character as he was already in the practise of his art? It is to be noted, as regards form, that one of Shelley's most consummate productions was inspired by the works and death of Keats. I doubt not that Keats's sensuous and matchless verse would have taken on, in time, more of the elusive spirituality for which we go to Shelley. As it was, he and Wordsworth were the complements of each other with their respective gifts, and made the way clear for Tennyson and his successors. Impressed by the supreme art and fresh imagination of the author of " Hyperion," not a few are disposed to award him a place on the topmost dais where but two English poets await his coming,—if not entitled there to an equal seat, at least with the right to stand beside the thrones as lineal inheritor, the first-born prince of the blood. His poetry has been studied with delight in this western world for the last half-century. One page of it is worth the whole product of the " æsthetic " dilettants who most recently have undertaken to direct us, as if by privilege of discovery, to the fountain-head of modern song. But

The One remains, the many change and pass.

This prophesying in the name of an acknowledged leader is old as the Christian era. And even the pagan Moschus, from whom, and from Bion, Shelley took the conception of his starry threnody, declares of a dead poet and certain live and unwelcome celebrants:

" Verily thou all silent wilt be covered in earth, while it has pleased the Nymphs that the frog shall always sing. Him, though, I would not envy, for he chants no beauteous strain."

V

LANDOR [1]

IF the many lovers of the beautiful, into whose
hands, we trust, this collection will fall, shall derive from the study of its gems something of the
pleasure experienced in their choice and arrangement,
the editors thus will be a second time rewarded for
most enjoyable labor. The master-artist, to whose
exquisite touch these compositions owe their excuse
for being, possessed beyond his contemporaries the
liberal faculty which endowed some of the great workmen of the past: the double gift upon which the poets,
sculptors, and painters of the golden age, before the
era of the specialists, were wont to plume themselves.
He had the joyous range of Benvenuto Cellini, whom
the chroniclers describe as " founder, gold-worker, and
medailleur "; who, in his larger moods, devised and
cast the Perseus and other massive bronzes which
still ennoble the Italian city-squares; yet who found
felicitous moments in which to carve the poniard-
handles, vaunted by knights and courtiers as their
rarest treasures, or to design some wonder of a cup,

[1] Introduction to *Cameos*. Selected from the works of Walter
Savage Landor by Edmund C. Stedman and Thomas Bailey
Aldrich. Boston: James R. Osgood & Company, 1873.

or bracelet, or other thing of beauty, for the queen or mistress of the monarch who protected him and honored his unrivalled art.

The legend of WALTER SAVAGE LANDOR justly might have been *Fineness and Strength,* since, while distinguished by his epic and dramatic powers, and at home in the domain of philosophic thought, he had also that delicate quality which enriches the smallest detail, and changes at will from its grander creations to those of subtile and ethereal perfection. He had the strongest touch and the lightest; his vision was of the broadest and the most minute. Leigh Hunt characterized him by saying that he had never known any one of such a vehement nature with so great delicacy of imagination, and that he was "like a stormy mountain-pine that should produce lilies." In this there is something of the universal genius of "men entirely great."

Landor's minor poems, therefore, bear a relation to his more extended work similar to that borne by Shakespeare's songs and sonnets to his immortal plays. Yet they are not songs, because not jubilant with that skylark gush of melody which made so musical the sunrise of English rhythm. They address themselves no less to the eye than to the ear; are the daintiest of lyrical idyls,—things to be seen as well as to be heard; compact of fortunate imagery, of statuesque conceptions marvellously cut in verse. Are we not right in designating them as *Cameos?* And from what other modern author could a selection of relievos be made, so flawless in outline and perfect in classical grace, for the delight of both the novice and the connoisseur?

So finished are these metrical carvings that the observer, mindful of the art *celare artem,* might suppose them to be the product of care and elaborate revision. But with Landor's lyrics, however it may be with those of the poets, it is known that the reverse was the case. He was a true improvisator,—and that, too, without recourse to the irregular freedom looked for in improvisations. The spontaneity of the early songsters, at least, was his; these little poems were the overflow of his genius, by means of which he relieved himself of a surplusage of passion, exhilaration, or scorn; and were thrown off with such ease and skill, both natural and acquired, that we are in doubt whether most to admire their beauty or the swift precision with which they grew to excellence beneath his hands.

Who has not chanced upon some lounging philosopher, retentive of his boyish or sea-faring skill, modelling with his penknife a ring or puzzle from a bit of wood,—possibly, a tiny basket from a nutshell,—while engaged in earnest argument; discoursing, it may be, of world-wide topics, and apparently almost unconscious of the work so deftly and gracefully responding to his artistic design? Just so it was Landor's habit while engaged upon his prose masterpieces, the *Imaginary Conversations,* the *Pentameron, Pericles· and Aspasia,*—or, in poetry, the noble *Helenics,*—to fashion at any hour or moment some delicious specimen of this cameo-work, without disturbing

[93]

the progress of his more intellectual and elevated creations.

One of the first qualities which should impress the reader of these verses is the thorough purity and simplicity of their English idiom. In prose and poetry, their author belonged to the school which clings to the natural order and genius of the English tongue, and in both departments of literature he easily ranked with the foremost. Nowadays, when there is so much of what is called word-painting, so much straining after effect through use of words painfully chosen for sound or color, it is difficult to estimate properly the limpid, translucent clearness of Landor's verse. It is Corinthian rather than Composite, and seems to disdain any resort to eccentric or meretricious devices. Doubtless its maker might have put words together as curiously as any imitator of a great poet's youthful style; but " doubtless," as Thomas Fuller would say, he " never did," however tempted by unlimited power of language, and with an exhaustless vocabulary at his control.

Though graven in the purest English, many of these gems reflect the manner of those Latin lyrists, with whom their author, in his gownsman days, became so familiar,—so imbued with their blithe and delicate spirit, that he may dispute with rare old Robert Herrick the title of the British Catullus. His epigrams are by turns playful and spleenful, and pointed as those of Martial; but among these, and in the lightness of his festive or amatory strains, there often is little of that emotion which takes the heart captive.

You are not moved to tears, as by the passion of
Mrs. Browning, the devotion and aspiration of Whittier, the pathos of Thomas Hood.   Many of them are,
as we have entitled them, just precious little works of
art; to be prized, studied, marvelled over,—like the
carved and mounted treasures of a virtuoso's collection,—for beauty, pure and simple, and the perfection
of their rhythmical execution.

Yet even in Tibullus there is nothing sweeter, and
little more touching and tender in the anthology of
our own tongue, than the stanzas composed by Landor
when his personal feelings really were claiming utterance.   As he laid bare his heart, whether in fiery
youth, or old and lonely as the oak that has outlived
its forest companions, he never gave voice to an un-
manly or pitiful complaint.   Yet, lion and eagle as
he was, he was not ashamed of the softest natural
emotion; it spontaneously broke out in his numbers;
the glitter of a tear is in many a line; there is a wandering echo in many a stanza which haunts the mind
long after.   Such is the charm of " Rose Aylmer," of
which it may be said that,—although it has happened
often that some minor lyric has entered the common
heart, and gained for an author that popular regard
which greater works have failed to procure him,—
there hardly is another instance in recent literature
where eight simple lines have so fascinated poetic and
sensitive natures.   Crabb Robinson recounts of Charles
Lamb, that, " both tipsy and sober, he is ever mutter-
ing ' Rose Aylmer ' "; and Lamb said, in his own
letter to Landor, " 'Tis for ' Rose Aylmer,' which has

a charm I cannot explain. I lived upon it for weeks."
The spell has been felt by many choice spirits, and
continues to this day; a letter before us, from one of
the most refined American essayists, says of Lamb's
extravagance: " Living on it for weeks is a daring
thing to say,—yet it is just what *I did.*" The Roses
of two later generations were dear to Landor for his
first love's sake, and, as we have embraced in this
collection other verses inspired by her beautiful memory, it will be seen how loyally and tenderly he clung
to it throughout the dreams and ventures of a prolonged, impulsive lifetime.

" Aglæ," " Aspasia to Cleone," " Pyrrha," and
other antiques, are to be found, strung along at intervals, in *Pericles and Aspasia,*—that unequalled
product of classical idealism, written in the most perfect English prose. Indeed, the conception of the
present volume arose from the statement in a recent
essay, that a book might be made of the lyrical gems
with which Landor's prose writings, even, are interspersed. " The Maid's Lament " is a ditty put into
the mouth of the youthful Shakespeare, in that remarkable Elizabethan study of the supposed Citation
of the future dramatist before Sir Thomas Lucy upon
a charge of deer-stealing. Some of the poet's lighter
stanzas are winsome for their careless, troubadour
spirit,—a mood not affected by him, but his sustainer
to the last; and our readers will not quarrel with us
for resetting " The One White Hair," " Sixteen,"
" Time to be Wise," familiar as these may be, on the
pages of the volume before them.

Speaking of "occasional" verses, Forster rightly says, that "the finest examples of such writings are often found in men who have also written poetry of the highest order." As Landor's trifles often were composed for the pleasure of exercising a natural gift, their fantasy of compliment or spleen was exaggerated to suit the poet's artistic caprice. He was not half so bitter as his epigrams pretended; was only "making believe," like some *vieux moustache* chaffing with a group of youngsters. When more in earnest, they served him as a safety-vent. One can hear the roar of laughter with which his rancor went to the winds, as he contemplated the imaginary flight of those at whom he aimed his winged shafts. In certain amatory verses, he really was more in love with his art than with its object. When he needed a heroine he took the nearest one, adorned her with regal expenditure, and invested her with the attributes of his own idea. There was the pretty Countess de Molandé, the Ianthe of his youth; in age, a sprightly and buxom Irish widow, with Landor still her devoted friend and cavalier. He used her as a lay-figure all his life, and dedicated lyrics to her that might have tempted a Vestal. No doubt she had as much appreciation of his songs as Lesbia for those of Catullus. Possibly she exclaimed, with Rosalind, "I never was so berhymed since Pythagoras' time"; yet thought no less of her minstrel, for was he not a rich and well-born Englishman, as handsome and robust a gallant as even an Irish beauty could desire? After all, his feeling for her was more than poetic affectation. There is something Quixotic in the regard of most poets for women, and having once determined that Dulcinea should be a princess, Landor persuaded himself that she was nothing less. Indeed, like Burns, he went to the extreme of chivalry with every woman he admired, and for the time was sincere in all the honors paid to her. How closely these two men,—one born in a cottage, the other inheriting an ancient name and estate,—were akin in their manly health, their free poetic vigor, their courtliness to women, their tenderness to children and animals, their sturdy and portentous defiance of bigots, charlatans, and snobs!

Landor's wit, especially in the sprightly rhymes of which his later years were prolific, occasionally was tinctured with the freedom of his Latin satirists; but rather in playful imitation of them than from any grossness in his own nature. It was a fault to write, and a still greater one to print, such verses; but it was the fault of that time of life when the faculty outstays the judgment. Of course, such indecorous trifles drew the attention and merciless censure of numberless Philistines, who chose to ignore, or were unconscious of the wisdom, goodness, and beauty of his serious literary achievements. In actual life he was a man without a vice, and whose every error might be traced to the infirmity of a most proud and obstreperous temper. Correct, temperate, and pure, he found a zest in outdoor communion with Nature, which maintained his inherent vitality to a grand old age. If his foibles subjected him to the charge of Paganism, his strength broke out in love of liberty, sympathy with the downtrodden, devotion to his honored poets and patriots, hatred of pretension and superstition. Among minor pieces which thus illustrate his character, their brevity and finish enable us to select the enduring verses to Browning, the lines upon Roland and Corday, and the tributes to Miss Mitford and Julius Hare.

Mrs. Browning declared Landor to be " of all living writers the most unconventional in thought and word, the most classical, because the freest from mere classicism, the most Greek, because pre-eminently and purely English." It seems to us that precisely the amount of benefit which a familiarity with the antique models can render to a modern poet is discernible in the greater portion of our selections. Their clearness and terseness are of the classic mould, but the language, thought, emotion, are Landorian and English. Of this twofold quality there are no better examples in our language than the companion-pieces, " To Youth " and " To Age." In finish these bear comparison with Collins's " Dirge in Cymbeline," and in feeling and purpose excel that melodious lyric. In respect to their theme, it may be said that no other poet has left so many or so beautiful verses inspired by the presence and sentiment of Age. Living long after he was content to die, he retained to the ninetieth year his sweetness of utterance and need for expression. It was the voice of Tithonus, whom Aurora had loved, thrilling tunefully and loudly after his bodily vigor had departed. It is said that poets die young; at all events the mass of poetry is ardent with the forward-looking hope of Youth; but in Landor's most felicitous strains he searches the brooding and pathetic memory of the past for imaginative suggestion, as one who has discovered that all Time is relative, and that to the poet who looks before and after there is no choice between the beginning and the end of days.

The reader has perceived that these introductory comments are restricted to the lyrical quality of Landor's genius, and to its productions, as displayed in the following exhibition. Our object having been to compose the latter solely of those faultless minor lyrics which come within the application of its title, of course many, and equally admirable, pieces are omitted. There is nothing in this volume which, from its length, severity, or freedom, will weary or repel the holder. Our intention has been to have it pure and charming, from the first selection to the end.

To many, these Cameos will present the graciousness of long familiar beauty, loveliest because best-remembered; to others, possibly, they may come as a first introduction to an author who only of late is beginning to be widely read, and whose works never have been placed fairly within the popular reach. To all such we offer this book in propitiation, assuring them that they are like wayfarers who have crossed the threshold of a royal, world-enriched Museum, and are examining a few of the more delicate treasures within its cabinets; glancing now at a carven sea-shell, and again at a winged head, cut upon agate or onyx for the finger of some beauty of the past; while around them are lofty walls laden with historical and dramatic paintings,—niches filled with statues of

heroes, heroines, and "many a fallen old Divinity,"—
and, in extended halls beyond, unique and changeful
panoramas depicting every country and time. In hope
that they will be led to look further for themselves,
we now invite them to examine these sculptured gems;
to note the hues of one, the matchless outlines of
another, and the satisfying grace and repose which
the hand of the same cunning artist has bestowed
upon them all.

VI

WILLIAM BLAKE, POET AND PAINTER[1]

IF Blake was not a great master, he had in him certain elements that go to the making of one. Often these were beyond his own control. One does not need to be a painter or a poet to see, in his extraordinary work, that he frequently was the servant rather than the master; that he was swept away, like his own Elijah, by the horses and chariot of fire, and that when, like Paul, he reached the third heaven—whether he was in the body or out of it, he could not tell. This was not so at all times. The conception and execution of his " Job " are massive, powerful, sublime, maintained throughout the series. " The Marriage of Heaven and Hell " is a wonderful, a fearlessly imaginative, production. But much of his labor with pen or pencil does not show that union of genius with method which declares the master. He does not always sit above the thunder; he is enrapt, whirled, trembling in the electric vortex of a cloud.

What is this, you say, but to be the more inspired? True, no man ever lived who had, at intervals, a more absolute revelation. He was obedient to the heavenly

[1] *The Critic,* January 15, 1881.

vision; but great masters, obeying it, find it in harmony with their own will and occasion. They have, moreover, the power to discern between false and foolish prophecies—between the monitions from a deity, and those from the limbo of dreams, delusions, and bewildered souls.

Did Blake see the apparitions he claimed to see? Did the heads of Edward and Wallace and the Man that built the Pyramids, rise at his bidding, like the phantoms summoned for Macbeth? I have no doubt of it. Neither, I think, will painters doubt it; for I suspect that they also have such visions,—they who are born with the sense that makes visible to the inward eye the aspect of forms and faces which they have imagined or composed, and with the faculty that retains them until the art of reproduction has done its service. We, who are not painters, at times see visions with our clouded eyes,—one face swiftly blotting out another, as if in mockery at our powerlessness to capture and depict them.

Men like Swedenborg and Blake, sensitive in every fibre and exalted by mysticism, accept as direct revelation the visions which other leaders understand to be the conceptions of their own faculty and utilize in the practice of their art.

One of Blake's masterly elements was individuality. His drawings are so original as to startle us; they seem like pictures from some new-discovered world, and require time for our just appreciation of their unique beauty, weirdness and power.

Another element was faith,—unbounded faith in his

religion, his mission, and the way revealed to him. To say that he had faith is to say also that he believed in himself; for his ecstatic piety and reverence and his most glorious visions were the unconscious effluence of his own nature. And that a poet or an artist should have faith is most vital and essential. He cannot be a mere agnostic. The leaders have had various beliefs, but each has held fast to his own. Take the lowest grade of Shakespeare's convictions: he believed in royalty and the divine right of kings. His kings, then, are chiefs indeed, hedged with divinity, and speaking in the kingliest diction of any language or time. If I were asked to name the most grievous thing in modern art, I should say it is the lack of some kind of faith. Doubt, distrust, the question, "What is the use?" make dim the canvas and burden many a lyre. The new faith looks to science and reign of law. Very well: these must breed its inspiration, as in time they will. But the processes of reason are slower than the childlike instincts of an early and poetic age.

Blake had the true gift of expression; he was not merely learned, but inventive, in his methods of drawing, etching, and color. Here, and in his talks concerning art, he showed power and wisdom enough to equip a host of ordinary draughtsmen. He was mad, only in the sense that gave the Clown warrant for saying all Englishmen are mad; only when he left the field in which he was thoroughly grounded, for speculations in which he was self-trained and half-trained. It is useless, however, to wonder what such an one might have been; he was what he was, and as great as he could be. There is no gainsaying his marvellous and instant imagination. He saw not the sunrise, but an innumerable company of the angelic host, crying, " Holy, holy, holy, is the Lord God Almighty! " Heaven and Hell are spirits, alike naked and alike clothed with beauty, rushing together in eternal love. Job and his friends are almost pre-Adamite in mould and visage. His daughters are, indeed, they of whom we are told, that there were not found others so fair in all the land. Jehovah himself came within Blake's vision; the dreamer walked, not only with sages and archangels and Titans, but with the very God.

Among his other qualities were a surprisingly delicate fancy, human tenderness and pity, industry and fertility in the extreme. He had ideas of right and government, and was grandly impatient of dulness and of hypocrisy in life or method. Finally, even his faults, and the grotesqueness which repeatedly brings his mark below the highest, add to the fascination that attends the revival and study of this artist. All that I say of his drawings applies in many respects to his rhymed and unrhymed verse. But his special gift was the draughtsman's. It would not be correct to say that he often hesitated with the pen, but never with the pencil, since, whether as an artist or as a maker of songs and " prophetic books," his product was bold and unstinted; but his grotesque errors are found more frequently in his poetry than in his designs, while his most original and exquisite range of verse is far below that attained by him in his works of outline and color.

These are the merest, the most fragmentary impressions of a man whom some have dismissed with a phrase, terming him a sublime madman, and concerning whom others—poets and critics of a subtle and poetic type—have written essay upon essay, or deemed whole volumes too brief for their glowing studies of his genius. If he did not found a school, it may almost be said that a modern school has founded itself upon the new understanding of his modes and purpose. But in copying the external qualities of Blake, it does not follow that his self-elected pupils are animated by his genius, rapture, and undaunted faith.

VII

WHITTIER [1]

IT would be unjust to consider Whittier's genius
from an academic point of view. British lovers
of poetry,—except John Bright and others of like
faith or spirit,—have been slow to comprehend his
distinctive rank. As a poet he was essentially a
balladist, with the faults of his qualities; and his
ballads, in their freedom, naïveté, even in their undue
length, are among our few modern examples of unsophisticated verse. He returned again and again to
their production, seldom laboring on sonnets and lyrics
of the Victorian mould. His ear for melody was
inferior to his sense of time, but that his over-facility
and structural defects were due less to lack of taste
than to early habit, Georgian models, disassociation
from the schools, is indicated by his work as a writer
of prose. In *Margaret Smith's Journal* an artistic,
though suppositive, Colonial style is well maintained.
Whittier became very sensible of his shortcomings;
and, when at leisure to devote himself to his art, he
greatly bettered it, giving much of his later verse all
the polish that it required. In extended composition,

---

[1] From the *Encyclopædia Britannica*, the Tenth and the
Eleventh Editions.

as when he followed Longfellow's *Tales of a Way-side Inn* with his own *The Tent on the Beach,* he often failed to rival his graceful brother poet. In American balladry he was pre-eminent; such pieces as " The Swan Song of Parson Avery," " Marguerite," " Barclay of Ury," " Skipper Ireson's Ride," " In the ' Old South,' " hold their place in literature. It is necessary above all to consider the relation of a people's years of growth and ferment to the song which represents them; for in the strains of Whittier, more than in those of any other nineteenth-century lyrist, the saying of Fletcher of Saltoun, as to the ballads and laws of a nation, finds historic illustration. He was the national bard of justice, humanity, and reform, whose voice went up as a trumpet until the victory was won. Its lapses resembled those of Mrs. Browning, who was of his own breed in her fervor and exaltation. To the last it was uncertain whether a poem by Whittier would " turn out a sang " or " perhaps turn out a sermon "; if the latter, it had deep sincerity and was as close to his soul as the other. He began as a liberator, but various causes employed his pen; his heart was with the people; he loved a worker, and the *Songs of Labor* convey the zest of the artisan and pioneer. From 1832 to 1863 no occasion escaped him for inspiring the assailants of slavery, or chanting pæans of their martyrdom or triumph. No crusade ever had a truer laureate than the author of " The Virginia Slave Mother," " The Pastoral Letter "—one of his stinging ballads against a time-serving Church, " A Sabbath Scene," and

"The Slaves of Martinique." "Randolph of Roanoke" is one of the most pathetic and elevated of memorial tributes. "Ichabod" and "The Lost Occasion," both evoked by the attitude of Webster, are Roman in their condemnation and "wild with all regret."

The green rusticity of Whittier's farm and village life imparted a bucolic charm to such lyrics as "In School Days," "The Barefoot Boy," "Telling the Bees," "Maud Muller," and "My Schoolmate." His idyllic masterpiece is the sustained transcript of winter scenery and home-life, *Snow-Bound*, which has had no equal except Longfellow's "Evangeline" in American favor, but, in fact, nothing of its class since "The Cottar's Saturday Night" can justly be compared with it. Along with the Quaker poet's homing sense and passion for liberty of body and soul, religion and patriotism are the dominant notes of his song. His conception of a citizen's prerogative and duty, as set forth in "The Eve of Election," certainly is not that of one whose legend is "our country, right or wrong." Faith, hope, and boundless charity pervade the "Questions of Life," "Invocation," and "The Two Angels," and are exquisitely blended in "The Eternal Goodness," perhaps the most enduring of his lyrical poems. "We can do without a Church," he wrote in a letter, "we cannot do without God; and of him we are sure." The inward voice was his inspiration, and of all American poets he was the one whose song was most like a prayer. A knightly celibate, his stainless life, his ardor, caused him to be termed a Yankee Galahad; a pure and simple heart was laid bare to those who loved him in " My Psalm," " My Triumph," and " An Autograph." The spiritual habit abated no whit of his inborn sagacity, and it is said that in his later years political leaders found no shrewder sage with whom to take counsel. When the question of primacy among American poets was canvassed by a group of the public men of Lincoln's time, the vote was for Whittier; he was at least one whom they understood, and who expressed their feeling and convictions. Parkman called him " The poet of New England," but as the North and West then were charged with the spirit of the New England states, the two verdicts were much the same. The facts remain that no other poet has sounded more native notes, or covered so much of the American legendary, and that Whittier's name, among the patriotic, clean and true, was one with which to conjure. He was revered by the people cleaving to their altars and their fires, and his birthdays were calendared as festivals, on which greetings were sent to him by young and old.

VIII

MR. BRYANT'S "THIRTY POEMS"[1]

THE pathetic outburst of Cato Major—"It is a hard thing, Romans, to render an account before the men of a period different from that in which one has lived!"—is a complaint which Mr. Bryant will never be constrained to imitate. His period is our own. While most of his noonday contemporaries have passed into neglect under the test of time, his poetry holds its assured position in the affections and judgment of the tasteful. It has a perennial charm. It is conceived in the abiding spirit of true art, subject in structure to the genius of our language, and is therefore not flat, stale, and unprofitable, when the fashion of the day, on which charlatans depend, has faded with the day itself.

His metres, and the sequences of his words, are those of Collins and Goldsmith and Cowper, and of all other English poets who have refused to depart from the natural order of English verse. To this order successive generations return with ever fresh delight, when wearied of the syllabub inventions whipped up in obedience to a craving for something original or new. And as the metre, so the thought

[1] *The Round Table*, January 16, 1864.

of Mr. Bryant. It is that which was old with the ancients, and is young in these later times—the pure philosophy of nature's lessons, the reflex of her visible forms.

Nor has Mr. Bryant's muse been restricted in her seldom flights to the petty limits of local scenery and fact. As befits a poet of this metropolis, his perception is catholic and has a broad horizon. Aloof from cliques, their influences have not confirmed him in his faults, nor led him to insensibly exaggerate the merits of his own vicinage and associates. The injurious effects of the converse situation painfully impress those who observe the self-constituted Mecca of our New England school. There, fine minds and noble characters have been dwarfed and warped by mutual flattery and cohesion. As they grow older, their crotchets are more crotchety, their poetry is less original, their philosophy more awry. But when Mr. Bryant writes of patriotism, he does not confine the splendor of its displays to Lexington and Concord, nor to the valor of a single tribe. His " Conqueror " is one who overcometh the world. His religion smacks of no university creed; and his sympathies are unnarrowed by either his political or æsthetic faith. Independent of any year or place, his verses should commend themselves, so long as the grass grows, and the water runs, and the winds breathe through the forests of the land in which he writes. If his affections have any local limit, it is one no less than his native country. For he is peculiarly an American poet.

In one sense, however, Mr. Bryant has a restricted range. There is little of human action in his productions; they are meditative, not dramatic, and invite us to observe the physical beauty of nature, rather than the clash of mind with mind, the currents of heart and heart. Herein they differ widely from the tendency of the age. But for lack of passion we are compensated by a surcharge of philosophic thought, the serene wisdom of a healthful soul discovering something far more deeply interfused in "all that we behold from this green earth."

These *Thirty Poems*, by their very tranquillity, will at first repel those who have been stall-fed on the seething excitement of the latest modes, and flattered to the top of their bent with the jingling variety of its cadences.

But give them another study, and their simplicity will have a most seductive charm. How easy it seems to write such natural lines! You would say that thoughts so familiar, verses so unadorned, must be commonplace. But learn to recognize the master-touch. We see bardlings who writhe before the oracle, striving how not to express themselves. Are their ideals profounder, or only more involved? The answer is plain. Clear thought makes clear language. Who sees brightly paints distinctive forms. When one declares he cannot utter his conception, he has not fully conceived. The faculty of human expression is divinely infinite. Mr. Bryant rarely goes beyond his sight and knowledge, and we say that the secret of his simplicity is his self-restraint. This is at once the safeguard of his poetry, of his prose, and of his almost blameless life.

We confess to feeling little of the critic's irreverence in reviewing this Nestor of our poets. Though long past the age at which his leading compeer now shows symptoms of declension, he returns to his first love, and has added to his metrical works a collection equal to about one-half their previous amount. Among the Thirty Poems are a few that have appeared elsewhere, but we read the greater portion for the first time. There are two entirely new and sustained pieces, each longer than any of his earlier works. We have also the Fifth Book of Homer's Odyssey, done into English blank-verse. The reader will perceive that this volume is the most important contribution which American poetry has for some years received.

The book opens with " The Planting of the Apple-Tree," now everywhere reprinted from magazine columns. This exquisite lyric affords an illustration of the limit to which Mr. Bryant, as a melodist, is subjected. With a purpose evidently to give spirited abruptness to the refrain, the last verse of each stanza is a foot shorter than its correspondent. This has a certain effect, but jars harshly on the even cadence of the author's style; and a more *facile* artist would have found a better way to achieve the desired result. When Mr. Bryant ventures beyond the established metres, it is with uncouthness and an air of doubt. He is in unknown waters, and would gladly touch firm land; but then, as we have said, he seldom ventures. The poem in question is followed by the perfectly beautiful "Snow Shower"; a little further on we have "Robert of Lincoln," full of bird music and delicate humor; and, toward the middle of the volume, the finely imaginative "Song of the Sower" teems with the richness of a fruitful theme. These four poems, though cast in moulds of the author's own devising, are, with the slight exception hitherto noted, in forms as well suited to the author's genius, because as evenly and nobly balanced, as those of his well-remembered "June" and "The Conqueror's Grave."

On page 79 we find the only inelegant expression of the book:

> Springs eagerly, and faintly sinks, *to where*
> The mother waters lie.

If there are any pieces which could have been omitted from this collection, they are, "An Invitation to the Country," the "Song for New Year's Eve," "The Wind and Stream," "These Prairies Glow with Flowers," and "The Mother's Hymn." It seems to us that many feebler singers might have printed these. Nor do the two poems evoked by the present war at all compare with that ringing clarion blast, "The Song of Marion's Men," which has stirred the pulses of every school-boy in the land, and to which no bugle but that of Motherwell could ever make response.

There are two simple and affluent forms of English verse in whose mastery Mr. Bryant is without an American rival. The first is the iambic quatrain,

of which a familiar stanza, " Truth crushed to Earth,"
in " The Battle-Field," may be cited as a specimen.
Perhaps the most finished poem of this volume is the
" Day-Dream." The poet sits by Posilippo's steep,
gazing at the bay, and recalling the olden time when
its sea-nymphs were visible to the clear, believing eye.
Witness such stanzas as these:

> I sat and watched the eternal flow
>   Of those smooth billows toward the shore,
> While quivering lines of light below
>   Ran with them on the ocean floor.

The Nereids rise before his view:

> Then moved their coral lips: a strain,
>   Low, sweet, and sorrowful, I heard,
> As if the murmurs of the main
>   Were shaped to syllable and word.

> *   *   *   *

> " Earth rears her flowers for us no more;
>   A half-remembered dream are we.
> Unseen we haunt the sunny shore,
>   And swim, unmarked, the glassy sea.

> *   *   *   *

> " Yet sometimes, as in elder days,
>   We come before the painter's eye,
> Or fix the sculptor's eager gaze,
>   With no profaner witness nigh.

> " And then the hearts of men grow warm
>   With praise and wonder, asking where
> The artist saw the perfect form
>   He copied forth in lines so fair?"

The second of the forms above-named is that blank verse of which Mr. Bryant's handling is always recognized. Setting aside the abuse of this noble English metre, exemplified in Young, Thompson, and a host of didactic writers, it is found in four distinct and luminous types. First, the Miltonic, in which Latin words and sonorous pauses and inversions predominate. This no one has satisfactorily written since the inventor whose name it bears. Second, the pure Heroic, modelled somewhat after the Greek, and largely indebted to Saxon words for its antique and epic vigor. Tennyson is a living master, and his " Morte d'Arthur " and " Idyls of the King " are leading examples, of this form. Third, the Shakespearean-Dramatic; and, lastly, the Reflective, of which Wordsworth had such high control. In the latter form, adapted to the poet's serenest and profoundest moods, Mr. Bryant has not been excelled. His imprint stamps every line which he has thus written. The " Thanatopsis " and " Forest Hymn " are embalmed in literature. Nor has his hand lost its cunning. In his new volume, " A Rain Dream," " The Night Journey of a River," and " The Constellations," are poems which none but Bryant could have written, and in his loftiest method. They are compact of high imaginings. Take, from the first, an impersonation of

—the wind of night:
A lonely wanderer between earth and cloud,
In the black shadow and the chilly mist,
Along the streaming mountain side, and through

The dripping woods, and o'er the plashy fields,
Roaming and sorrowing still, like one who makes
The journey of life alone, and nowhere meets
A welcome or a friend, and still goes on
In darkness.

The pieces to which we have alluded, as the longest in the book, " Sella " and " The Little Children of the Snow," as well as the translation from Homer, are also in blank verse. The first two, in their pure, artistic interest, present a marked contrast to that rhythmical essay, " The Ages," which is the first in date and extent, and the least in value, of Mr. Bryant's former productions.

" Sella " occupies thirty-two delicious pages. It is a story of

—the days of old,
The days when there were goodly marvels yet,

of a maiden living near a streamlet whose current had a mystic charm to woo her. She haunted some lake or river from morn till night, loving the waters, and yearning for a knowledge of the great sea. One day a marvellous pair of slippers, inscribed with her name, are found upon the streamlet's brink. When she puts them on she can fearlessly plunge beneath the current, and follow its windings to the ocean, in whose recesses she meets, and learns to love, the blissful creatures of the deep. She returns to her cottage-home; but as time rolls on her absences are frequent and longer. At last her brothers resolve to stop such practices, espy the hiding-place of the slippers, steal them, and return them to the eager brook. The gods give not their favors twice, and Sella was for ever banished from her dearer life, but became a benefactress of the upper world. When she died,

> A hundred cities mourned her, and her death
> Saddened the pastoral valleys.

" The Little People of the Snow " is a sweet eclogue, wherein Uncle John tells a fairy tale to Alice: a story of a little mountain maid who was tempted by the snow-elves to roam beyond limits set by her parents, and who saw the myriad wonders of the crystal world, but at last perished, chilled to death with the very hospitality of her colder-blooded companions. Since Eva's burial,

>   —never more
> The little people of the snow were seen
> By human eyes,   *   *   *   *
> For a decree went forth to cut them off,
> For ever, from communion with mankind.

The verse of these two poems is light and graceful, melodiously adapted to their themes, and greatly modified from Mr. Bryant's reflective style. They are imaginative throughout, but especially attractive for the rare fancy which sparkles in every line. The author's heart seems budding with a greenness which it somewhat lacked in the springtime of his life, and thus, by natural piety, could we also wish our days " bound each to each."

A few comments on his version of the Fifth Odyssey. A new Homeric translation is always of novel interest. No rendering has been thoroughly successful. Chapman's version, though "loud and bold," is too often careless and obscure. Pope's flowing couplets are anything but a translation. Cowper's unrhymed efforts are preferable, but the bard of Olney lost all his simplicity, and became turgid and involved, laden with those stronger measures than his own. Critics vary with regard to the merits of Sotheby, Newman, Mumford, and the rest. There is room and a welcome for a truly meritorious version of the Homeric poems.

We do not think that a complete translation, after the manner of Mr. Bryant, would supply this want. In a note, justly censuring the stiff inversions of Cowper, he says: " Homer, of course, wrote in idiomatic Greek, and, in order to produce either a true copy of the original, or an agreeable poem, should have been translated into idiomatic English." True, but Homer's idioms are those of the Epic (early Ionic) dialect—as far apart, in construction and word-formation, from the Attic, or the polished later Ionic, as the text of Chaucer is from that of Pope. The poems of Homer, however, unlike those of our early English bards, are in a measured and exactly finished, though antique verse; their faultless art filling every appreciative reader with delight, and rendering them patent to all time. Now Mr. Bryant has succeeded, first, in presenting a literal version of the Greek, and, second, in forcing his verse translation to assume the modern

English synthesis. We have compared a few passages with the original, and are struck with their fidelity. Few words are added or omitted, and the sense is generally correct. But the very success of the translator's second intention has the effect of commonplace. Take the opening of the book:

> Aurora, rising from her couch beside
> The famed Tithonus, brought the light of day
> To men and to immortals. Then the gods
> Came to their seats in council. With them came
> High thundering Jupiter, amongst them all
> The mightiest. Pallas, mindful of the past,
> Spoke of Ulysses and his many woes,
> Grieved that he still was with the island nymph.

This exordium verges on the prosaic. Homer says the same thing, and in about the same space; but the stately choice and order of his language lift it to the dignity of epic verse. Another instance: the line,

> Ulysses, the sagacious, answered her,

is a meagre substitute for the resonant and courtly

Τὴν δ' ἀπαμειβόμενος προσέφη πολύμητις 'Οδυσσεύς.

Mr. Bryant's version loses the essential quality of *rest,* which makes the antique song carry us ever forward without palling to the ear. The genius of the Homeric ballad, like that of a skilfully managed fantasia, is to return incessantly to the " theme," and, after the longest and loftiest flights, by a recurrence to the refrain, to prepare the listener for another rapture. In the monotonous interludes, which always introduce the same personage in the same language, there is a just scorn of varying light mechanic matters when a noble subject is in hand.

The Olympian hierarchy will not forgive Mr. Bryant for converting their high-sounding names into Latin equivalents. In fact, that characteristic of his style which most unfits it for translation of the Greek is its Latinism. It was impossible for the Romans to catch and reproduce the Hellenic spirit. We have no sympathy with the cant which deprecates the use of those Latin words by which our language is most enriched; but it is a fact that the Greek is best expressed by authors who rely chiefly on the Saxon, and that there is a singular harmony between the effects of the Greek and Saxon verse. To conclude: Homer will never receive an adequate translation; but the method which indicates itself as the nearest means thereto, is that of the aforesaid pure-Heroic blank-verse. The latter is full of Saxon strength, adapting itself to the sonorous refrain, and constructed in that epic order of words which is as natural to one century as to another. Probably the " Morte d'Arthur " of Tennyson, and Matthew Arnold's " Balder Dead," are the best specimens of this method in our language.

With Spanish poetry Mr. Bryant is entirely successful. His verse renders the grave Roman feeling of the Castilian muse to our outer and inner senses. Every reader will be repaid by a study of that Latinesque production, " The Ruins of Italica "; and " The Lost Bird " (by Carolina Colorado de Perry) is suggestive and melodious as the Spanish lyric itself.

Throughout the volume are evidences of a serene and joyous prime, which age cannot wither, nor the rust of years corrode. " The Life that Is," " A Sick Bed," " The New and the Old," " The Cloud on the Way," are all recognitions of the season to which the singer and his life-companions have arrived; but they breathe compliance with the sweet law of Nature's successions, and are radiant with faith that looks beyond the vail. His philosophy, like his poetic art, resembles a tranquil river still widening toward the close.

And now, in a brief and merely suggestive review, how little fault we have been able to find with these *Thirty Poems!* Their excellences have grown upon us; for their author incases himself in proof, and is open to few charges, save that of being " faultily faultless." They have the effect of Kensett's pictures—cool, rich, dark, satisfying, a welcome relief from the feverish midday glare, the shadow of a great rock in a weary land. With all this, such a burden of rhymes now loads the press, that it is doubtful whether, if Mr. Bryant were for the first time craving the public suffrage, he would assume a central position in the hemicycle of our poets. For the unusual, not the noblest, is in vogue. It was much for him to have commenced in that fallow-period of American literature, when any writer was noticeable; and fortunate that his sure excellence thus reached the foreground, where all pause to catch the deep sound of his chanting. To you, who have yet your laurels to win, and would fain win them purely, what heart-searching years of inappreciation and neglect! Your task is harder than his. But approach the altar with his reverent step; be simple, conscientious, impassioned, assured of the goal. Thus you, he says, may also

> Frame a lay
> That haply may endure from age to age,
> And they who read shall say:
> What witchery hangs upon this poet's page!
> What art is his, the written spells to find
> That sway from mood to mood the willing mind!

IX

MR. BRYANT'S "HOMER" [1]

IN completion of his Homeric labors, Mr. Bryant now gives us the translation of a work which, although composed in the very diction of the Iliad, varies widely from that poem in feeling, material, and theme. The two epics do not differ as "Paradise Regained," for instance, differs from "Paradise Lost." The Odyssey is correlative to the Iliad, and, in its own way, not inferior. The latter is all fire and action, portraying superbly barbaric manners and glorying in the right of might alone: a succession of lyrical passages, thrown together much at random, which rehearse the councils and warfare of men and gods, and are strong with passion and the noble imagery of an heroic age. The Odyssey has that unity which the Iliad lacks. Its structural purpose, to recount the wanderings of Ulysses, is evenly carried through to the appointed end. Manifestly a somewhat later work, it hints at the repose of civilization, and is almost idyllic in tone. After rising to epic fury, as in the slaying of the suitors, it hastens, regardless of anti-climax, to the scenes and dialogue of pastoral life. In it we see less of "Olympus'

---

[1] *The Atlantic Monthly*, May, 1872.

hierarchy " than in the Iliad, and more of the nymphs and demigods who dwell on earth and haunt the ways of men. Otherwise considered, the Odyssey is Eastern, almost arabesque; a piece of wonder-lore; a tale of enchantments; a magical journey, involving the real and ideal geography of the ancient world. It moves from island to island, and from town to town, never straying far from the ocean; delighting to visit many peoples and to cleave the hoary brine.

It would seem natural for the poet of our own forests and waters to find himself more in sympathy with the spirit of the Odyssey; yet, in his translation of the Iliad, Mr. Bryant entered, as if endowed with new and dramatic inspiration, upon the fervid action of the martial song. He now tells us that, executing his present task, he has " certainly missed in the Odyssey the fire and vehemence of which " he " was so often sensible in the Iliad, and the effect of which was to kindle the mind of the translator." We will look for compensation to those exquisite descriptive passages, which, scattered through the Odyssey, stimulate the copyist to put forth all his powers. As Mr. Bryant's version of the Iliad was greatest where most strength and passion were required, so we observe that in the selectest portions of the Odyssey he warms up to his work, and is never finer than at a critical moment. The reader of these volumes will be charmed with the perfect grace and beauty of many scenic descriptions, where the translator's command of language seems most enlarged, and the measure flows with the rhythmic perfection of his original poems.

Take, for illustration, an extract from the passage in the Fifth Book, familiar through the verse of many English minstrels, who have not essayed a complete reproduction of the Homeric songs :—

> But when he reached that island far away,
> Forth from the dark-blue ocean-swell he stepped
> Upon the sea-beach, walking till he came
> To the vast cave in which the bright-haired nymph
> Made her abode.   He found the nymph within;
> A fire blazed brightly on the hearth, and far
> Was wafted o'er the isle the fragrant smoke
> Of cloven cedar, burning in the flame,
> And cypresswood. Meanwhile, in her recess,
> She sweetly sang, as busily she threw
> The golden shuttle through the web she wove.
> And all about the grotto alders grew,
> And poplars, and sweet-smelling cypresses.
> In a green forest, high among whose boughs
> Birds of broad wing, wood-owls, and falcons built
> Their nests, and crows, with voices sounding far,
> All haunting for their food the ocean-side,
> A vine, with downy leaves and clustering grapes,
> Crept over all the cavern rock.   Four springs
> Poured forth their glittering waters in a row,
> And here and there went wandering side by side.
> Around were meadows of soft green, o'ergrown
> With violets and parsley.   'Twas a spot
> Where even an immortal might awhile
> Linger, and gaze with wonder and delight.

This is far more literal than the favorite translation by Leigh Hunt, and excels all others in ease and choice of language. The following extract will show how effectively Mr. Bryant substitutes, for the Greek color

and swelling harmony, the gloom and vigor of our
Saxon tongue:—

> The steady wind
> Swelled out the canvas in the midst; the ship
> Moved on, the dark sea roaring round her keel,
> As swiftly through the waves she cleft her way.
> And when the rigging of that swift black ship
> Was firmly in its place, they filled their cups
> With wine, and to the ever-living gods
> Poured out libations, most of all to one,
> Jove's blue-eyed daughter. Thus through all that night
> And all the ensuing morn they held their way.

The general characteristics of Mr. Bryant's Odyssey
are those which have rendered eminent his translation
of the Iliad,—fidelity to the text; genuine simplicity
of thought and style; successful transfusion of the
heroic spirit; above all, a purity of language which is,
from first to last, a continual refreshment to the
healthy-minded reader. The diction is not copious,
neither—in a modern sense—was that of Homer; and
there is no lack of minstrels, nowadays, who ransack
their vocabularies to fill with " words, words," our
jaded ears. As a presentment of English undefiled,
the value of this translation is beyond cavil. Indeed,
a main distinction of its author is that he belongs to
the natural, abiding school. He does not consider too
curiously, nor mistake suggestion for imagination; and
his style is of that quality which, as vogue after vogue
has its day, and the world cries out for a new departure, may often serve as a standard by which to gauge
the integrity of our poetic art.

The simplicity of his manner is unaffected. It is *simplicité*, not *simplesse*,—the distinction between which has been illustrated by Professor Arnold in a comparison of Wordsworth and Tennyson. There is, it seems to us, much that is common to the genius of the Homeric poems and that of their present translator,—a broad and general way of regarding man and nature, a largeness of utterance, and an imagination always luminous and sufficient to the theme.

The office of a translator is now well understood. It is, to reproduce literally the matter of his author, and to convey the manner and movement to the utmost extent permitted by the limitations of his own tongue. Until the latter has been accomplished, there is always room and a welcome for new effort. Respecting Mr. Bryant's Odyssey we can affirm that he has gone beyond his predecessors. He has equalled, and generally excelled, the literalness of Cowper, and, so far as manner is concerned, has achieved a better general effect than Chapman, Pope, or Worsley. Yet Worsley's Spenserian version has many delightful features. In view of the romantic nature of the Odyssey, it was a happy thought to render it into the graceful mediæval stanza: a verse redolent with the sensuous enchantment of a period when half the world was yet unknown, when personal adventure and travel were the desire of youth and age, and the chosen measure of Spenser was the medium of their poetic narration. It is slow to pall upon the senses, and Worsley has handled it deliciously. But in his Odyssey the matter is constantly sacrificed to the translator's art, and

[129]

the whole effect is Elizabethan rather than Homeric.

Nothing can be more clear and fascinating than Mr. Bryant's narrative, conveyed in the true epic manner with regard to directness and nobility of style. In striking passages, whose original beauty is high-sounding and polysyllabic, he most frequently obtains a corresponding English effect by reliance upon the strength of monosyllabic words:—

> For his is the black doom of death, ordained
> By the great gods.
>   Hear me yet more:
> When she shall smite thee with her wand, draw forth
> Thy good sword from thy thigh and rush at her
> As if to take her life, and she will crouch
> In fear.
>   I hate
> To tell again a tale once fully told.

But occasionally he uses to advantage the Latinism peculiar to his reflective poems. Such lines as Shakespeare's,

> The multitudinous seas incarnadine,

show by what process the twin forces of our English tongue are fully brought in play. Verses of this sort, formed by the juxtaposition of the numerous Greek particles with ringing derivative and compound words, make up the body of the Homeric song. Mr. Bryant accordingly varies his translation with lines which remind us of " Thanatopsis " or " A Forest Hymn ":—

The innumerable nations of the dead.
That strength and these unconquerable hands.
And downward plunged the unmanageable rock.

His paraphrases of the Greek idioms are noticeable for English idiomatic purity, so much so that the idea of a translation frequently absents itself from the reader's mind. While in one respect this is the perfection of such work, in another it is the loss of that indefinable charm pertaining to the sense of all rare things which are foreign to our own mode and period. His self-restraint, also, is carried to the verge of sterility by the repetition of certain adjectives as the equivalents of Greek words varying among themselves. The words " glorious " and " sagacious," for example, not uncommon in this translation, do not always represent the same, or even synonymous expressions in the original text. But most of Mr. Bryant's epithets and renderings—such as " the large-souled Ulysses," " the unfruitful sea," " passed into the Underworld," and his retention of Cowper's noble paraphrase of $\gamma\acute{\epsilon}\rho\omega\nu$ $\ddot{a}\lambda\iota os$, " the Ancient of the Deep "—give an elevated and highly poetical tone to the whole work. The modern translator of Homer possesses a great advantage in the establishment of the text and the concordance of scholars upon the interpretation of obscure passages; but we find evidence that Mr. Bryant often has looked to the primitive meaning of a word, the result being some original and felicitous rendering.

The exquisitely written Preface to this volume contains a forcible argument in defence of the author's retention of those Roman names by which the deities of Grecian mythology have been popularly known. Mr. Bryant's decision is in keeping with the habit of his mind, and highly authoritative, yet we trust that our regret that it should have been thus given does not savor of pedantry. We suspect that book-lovers, of the rising generation, are more familiar than he conceives them to be with the Hellenic proper names. They could not well be otherwise, reading Grote, Tennyson, and the Brownings, not to include Swinburne and the younger host of poets at home and abroad. And if Lord Derby in England, and Mr. Bryant in America, had adopted that nomenclature which, after all, is the only truthful one, the transition would have been complete, and the existing confusion brought to a conclusive end.

We have paid homage to the excellence of this translation, and briefly endeavored to show in what its power and beauty consist. It seems eminently proper that its author should have adopted blank-verse as the measure for his use. The English reader is wonted to this verse as the metre for a sustained epic poem. Probably in no other, at this stage of our poetic art, can the text of Homer be so faithfully rendered and his manner so nearly reached. It is the one, above all others, in which Mr. Bryant, its born master, was sure to achieve success. Finally, no blank-verse translation, at all commensurate with the limits of this stately measure, has hitherto been given us. There was a void which needed filling, but it

exists no longer. Had Mr. Tennyson undertaken the
full translation of Homer, after the manner indicated
by that magnificent early production, the "Morte
d'Arthur," we are sure that something very fine would
have been the result. Bryant's verse is noticeably
different from that of Tennyson. Only in an occasional passage, like the following, the one reminds us
of the other:—

> The formidable baldric, on whose band
> Of gold were sculptured marvels,—forms of bears,
> Wild boars, grim lions, battles, skirmishings,
> And death by wounds, and slaughter.

But Mr. Tennyson himself would be the first now to
recognize the fact that a great blank-verse translation
has been written, and that for another there can be
no well-founded demand.

A point still remains unsettled, even by the work
under review. Are we prepared to assert that all has
been done which can be done to represent Homer to
the English ear? The question which Mr. Bryant
put to himself was, not whether the Greek epics could
be adequately translated, for that can never be, but
whether the resources of the language afford any
better medium for their translation than that of heroic
blank-verse. This he has decided in the negative,
giving his reasons therefor; and the argument on that
side is further extended by Mr. Lewis in a brilliant
review of Bryant's Iliad and the nature of the Homeric
poems.

Many, with even a superficial knowledge of the
Greek text, will confess that, while delighted with the
unequalled merits of this translation, they still are
conscious of something yet to be achieved. What is
the one thing wanting? We have intimated that its
absence is least felt in those elevated passages, the
fiery glow of which for a time lifts us above contemplation of the translator's art. But in the more
mechanical portions blank-verse cannot of itself, by
the music and flexibility of its structure, have the
converse effect of holding us above the level of the
theme. Here the deficiency is felt. And for this
reason, amongst others, that in Greek the names of the
most common objects are imposing and melodious.
Hence those lines whose poverty of thought is greatest,
upborne by the long roll of the hexameter, have a
quality as aristocratic as the grace and dignity of a
Spanish beggar. Undoubtedly Mr. Bryant has perceived the weakness of blank-verse in those intercalary
lines, which are such a feature in Homer, and constitute a kind of refrain, affording rest at intervals
along the torrent of the song. In the best lyric and
epic poetry of all nations a disdain of minor changes
is observable; but Mr. Bryant, seeing that blank-verse
does little honor to a purely mechanical office, often
has varied his translations of such lines, instead of
following the Homeric method of recurrence to one
chosen form. The very directness of his syntax, leading to the rejection, even, of such inversions as Tennyson's,

To whom replied King Arthur, much in wrath,

has made it almost prosaic in this respect. Such lines
as

> Telemachus, the prudent, thus rejoined
> And then discreet Telemachus replied
> Ulysses, the sagacious, answered her

are tame substitutes for the courtly and sonorous
interludes,

> Τὴν δ' αὖ Τηλέμαχος πεπνυμένος ἀντίον ηὔδα·
> Τὴν δ' ἀπαμειβόμενος προσέφη πολύμητις Ὀδυσσεύς·

and lower the poetical tone of the general translation.
We feel still more the indefinite shortcomings of blank-
verse in the paraphrases of those resonant dactylic
lines, which make up so large a portion of the Iliad
and Odyssey, and give splendor to the movement of
whole cantos. We might cite innumerable examples,
like the following:—

> Ἦμος δ' ἠριγένεια φάνη ῥοδοδάκτυλος Ἠώς.

> But when the Morn,
> The rosy-fingered child of Dawn, looked forth.

> Μήνιος ἐξ ὀλοῆς Γλαυκώπιδος ὀβριμοπάτρης,
> Ἥτ' ἔριν Ἀτρείδῃσι μετ' ἀμφοτέροισιν ἔθηκεν

> The fatal wrath of her,
> The blue-eyed maid, who claims her birth from Jove.
> 'Twas she who kindled strife between the sons
> Of Atreus.

Αὐτὰρ ἐπεὶ ποταμοῖο λίπεν ῥόον Ὠκεανοῖο
Νηῦς, ἀπὸ δ' ἵκετο κῦμα θαλάσσης εὐρυπόροιο.

Now when our bark had left Oceanus
And entered the great deep.

All this points to the one deficiency in a blank-verse translation, and this, unquestionably, relates to the *movement*. Can a version in our slow and stately iambics, which are perfectly adequate to represent the dialogue of the Greek dramas, approximate to the rhythmic effect of a measure which originally was chanted or intoned? The rush of epic song has been partially caught by Chapman, Pope, and others, at the expense of both matter and style; and it may be owing to the pleasure afforded by this quality, that Pope's translation has held so long the regard of English readers. But only in one instance, that we now recall, has modern blank-verse attained to anything like the Homeric swiftness. A study of the tournament-scene, which closes the Fifth Book of " The Princess," will show to what we refer; yet even the splendid movement of this passage is unrestful, and like the fierce spurt of a racer that can win by a dash, but has not the bottom needed for a three-mile heat.

There are two forms of English verse in which, we think, the Homeric *rhythmus* may be more nearly approached. A good objection has been made to our rhymed heroic measure, as used by Pope (and by Dryden in his Virgil), that it disturbs the force of the original by connecting thoughts not meant to be connected; that it causes a " balancing of expression in

the two lines of which it consists, which is wholly
foreign to the Homeric style." Professor Hadley
has suggested that this may be obviated by a return
to the measure as written by Chaucer, not pausing too
often at the rhymes, but frequently running the sen-
tences over, with the cæsura varied as in blank-verse.
This usage, in fact, was revived by Keats and Leigh
Hunt, and is notable, of late, in William Morris's
flowing poetry, to which Mr. Hadley refers for illustration. Chapman translated the Odyssey upon this
plan, but in a slovenly fashion, not to be compared with
his other Homeric work. There is room, perhaps, for
a new translation of Homer into the rhymed Chau-
cerian verse.

Lastly, and at the risk of losing the regard of the
reader who may have gone with us thus far, we have
a word to say in behalf of that much-abused form of
verse known as the " English hexameter ": a measure
far more out of favor with the critics than with the
poets or the majority of their readers. Before its
name even was known in this country to other than
scholars, Mr. Longfellow's " Evangeline " appeared,
and found its way to the public heart as no American
poem of equal length ever had done before. Our
people made no difficulty in reading it, troubling themselves very little with the strictures of classical re-
viewers, and it has not yet outlived its original welcome.

The fact is that, to properly estimate the so-called
English hexameter, one must, to a certain extent, get
the Greek and Latin quantities out of his mind. Pro-

fessor Arnold and Mr. Lewis, among the rest, have contributed to the discussion on this subject, the one for, and the other against, the employment of hexameter in translation. Neither of them, it seems to us, succeeds in looking at the question from an independent point of view. Mr. Arnold would have our hexameter more spondaic and classical. Mr. Lewis sees that it cannot be written classically, but does not abuse it much on that account. He says that " it is peculiar among English metres, because it is so very like prose. It is less metrical than any form of English verse. Blank-verse," he adds, " can stoop to the simplest speech without approaching prose." True, but it does not always do so. Run together the opening lines of Mr. Bryant's Odyssey, which in Greek are made highly poetical by the structure and sound, and see if they have not a somewhat prosaic effect :—

" Tell me, O Muse, of that sagacious man who, having overthrown the sacred town of Ilium, wandered far and visited the capitals of many nations, learned the customs of their dwellers, and endured great suffering on the deep."

Now where, in Mr. Kingsley's " Andromeda,"—a fair specimen of English hexameter, with exquisite cadences throughout,—can five lines be made to read like that? Mr. Bryant has made the most of his material; the barrenness is in the verse.

No master of the natural English hexameter has yet arisen who has brought it to the perfection which charms both scholars and laymen; no translation of Homer has been made which affords any assistance

[138]

to our side of the argument by surpassing the excellence of Mr. Bryant's work. Asserting, then, that he has achieved a triumph in the only direction open at this period, we nevertheless venture to predict, that a resonant, swift metre will be developed, from elements now felt by our best poets to exist, which will have six accentual divisions, and hence may be called English hexameter verse; that it will partake of the quantitative nature of the intoned classical measures only through those natural dactyls not uncommon in our tongue, and through a resemblance which some of our trochees bear to the Greek spondaic feet; that it will be so much the more flexible, giving the poet liberty to shift his accents and now and then prefix redundant syllables; finally, that it often will have the billowy roll of the classical hexameter (as we moderns read the latter accentually), and by its form will be equal to the reproduction of Homer, line for line. If Mr. Taylor, who, by argument and practice, has proved the value of Form to the translator's work, can reach so near his mark in rendering the hundred metres of "Faust," surely there is encouragement for a future attempt to represent more closely the one defiant measure of heroic song. To the point made that English is too consonantal for such representation, we reply that it is no more consonantal in hexameter than in pentameter verse, and that, of the two kinds, the former is nearer to the verse of Homer. This objection would apply more forcibly to the still harsher German; yet we conceive Voss's Iliad to have given German readers a truer idea of the original than any English translation has yet conveyed to ourselves.

Such a metre, then, will be added to our standard verse-forms. It will be accepted by poets and critics, and the world will read it, arguing no more of dactyls and spondees than it now argues of iambics in blank-verse. Nor will any new English Homer tread upon the renown of Mr. Bryant's crowning work, until the English hexameter—with all its compensating qualities, by which alone we can preserve delicate shades of meaning and the epic movement—has been firmly established among us, and a great poet, imbued with the classical spirit, has become its acknowledged master.

Until then, Mr. Bryant's noble translation has filled the literary void. A host of English readers will long return to it with admiration and delight. Let us revere and cherish the fame of our eldest bard. He still remains among us, unchanged and monumental, surrounded by the unsettled, transitional art of the later generation,—as some Doric temple remains, in a land where grotesque and artificial structures have sprung up for a time,—an emblem of the strength of a more natural period, teaching the beauty of simplicity, and the endurance of that which is harmonious and true.

X

STODDARD'S POEMS [1]

FOR some time past our Miltons of the Atlantic coast have been mute, if not inglorious, taking silent observation of the new departure indicated by the present lyrical vogue. They have shrunk away before the outburst of gulch-and-canyon minstrelsy— somewhat as high tragedians take to their beds when the coming of Ixion is announced; or, it may be, are in their respective strongholds, burnishing their arms for a victorious return to the tournament of song. Meantime the crown has been yielded to our rampant knights of the West, who, each bestriding a mustang more untamed than his predecessors, have tilted over the lists—one or two of them by way of recreation from service of another kind. We have heard the sound of their publishers' heraldic trumpetings and the plaudits of the multitude below the tiers—and on the head of each in turn we have seen

> Perfume and flowers fall in showers
> That lightly rain from ladies' hands.

Thus it ever has been the wide world over. The lists are open to all knights, errant or otherwise; and they

[1] *The World,* New York, November 3, 1871.

[141]

who have won old triumphs may be sure that, if they
hoard their fame too long, the newer aspirant—though
not, perchance, the nobler—will become the favorite
of the day.

Mr. Stoddard is the first of our Eastern poets to
break the spell of their prolonged reserve. Many will
choose to regard the title of his new volume as an
intentional counterpoise to the popular mode, and as
a pronunciamento of his own estate, fealty, and inspiration. It is derived, however, from a collection
of those Oriental lyrics, to one of which we never
listen without desiring to paraphrase the refrain in the
Arabian Knights and say: " Pray sing us another of
those love-songs which you know how to sing so well! "
These elegant versions from the Persian, Tartar, and
Chinese poetry, rendered with subtle and delicate
touch, occupy the closing pages of *The Book of the
East*. Taken separately they vary in merit and interest; but together they form a beautiful rose-garden,
filled with flowers of both lustrous and sombre hues.
We are glad to see them here, as they exhale the per-
fume of their author's earlier work and gracefully
invite us to an acquaintance with the stronger and more
elevated poems by which they are preceded.

Mr. Stoddard holds a place of honor amongst the
few acknowledged American poets who stand half-
way between the elder and new generations, and may
be reckoned as at the prime of his powers. It is some
fifteen years, we think, since he last made a collection
of his minor poetry. Many of the pieces in this volume
have appeared during the interval, and not long ago

The King's Bell—the most extended and beautiful of his narrative productions—was issued by itself, and at once found a lasting place in the admiration of select lovers of poetry. On the whole, it seems to us that Mr. Stoddard has been somewhat careless of fame, as indeed a poet living in New York is apt to be. In provincial cities, where there is little enough to see, desire grows upon us to be seen and known of all men; but in the metropolis, where one can see so much and be himself so easily lost from public sight, a philosophic artist soon realizes that his own greater or less renown is of little moment compared with the storm and progress of the life about him. Once impressed with this feeling, his solicitude for appreciation is merged in love for art itself, unless, forsooth, he be stimulated by some publisher akin to that bearded husband of the ballet dancer in *Hyperion* who says: "I shall run her six nights at Munich, and then take her on to Vienna." For a poet of true sensibility never can run himself, even with a stage name plagiarized from a "grizzly" and a stage pair of seven-league top-boots.

The *Songs of Summer,* to which we have alluded, was Stoddard's second contribution, in book-form, to our metrical literature, and was composed of songs and idyls written after he had outgrown the undue influence of his early models (albeit these were of the best), and his genius had developed its specific quality. In fact, quality breathed from every leaf of that book, and at this day there is no single volume of American poetry to which, as a whole, we recur more often or with more pleasure. Its beautiful succession of lyrics, thrown off in a style thoroughly his own—all compact of wild and witching music, full as Shelley's of sudden cadences and dying falls, and spontaneous as the carols of the Elizabeth songsters—were each a work of melodious English art. They so dwelt upon the ear as to draw attention from the more extended compositions of which they were the overture. " The Abdication of Noman the Elder " is a masterpiece. " The Fisher and Charon "—a classical production of some length—as an example of noble and sustained blank-verse has not been excelled, in our way of thinking, by any American poem. It is stately, Doric, and imaginative to a high degree.

A book of the East should represent the meridian of age, experience, and culture. What may we fairly demand from an Eastern poet? First, the genius that should inform a poet of whatever clime or period; secondly, a breadth of training and thought, not only enabling him to equal the poet of a newer region in the latter specialty, but giving him a poly-sided skill to excel in many specialties. He must touch life through and through and all around—" best bard because the wisest." It is time to estimate by some such high test a poet whose home is that portion of this New World which, to regions westward, has already become the Old.

In *The Book of the East* we accordingly find that Stoddard retains his lyrical faculty and technical skill, and we also discover that he composes not merely from the love of faultless execution, but with the thoughtful inspiration of maturity. The book is more subjective than his former work. The converse is true of many poets, who seem only in youth—when the secrets of their emotion are least worth knowing —to remember Sidney's injunction, " Look in thy heart and write."

Stoddard avowedly belongs to the natural, universal school. Rejecting the idea that a cisatlantic poet should imitate the inventor of corn-stalk architecture, and adopt new modes less excellent than those already tested, he believes that an artist has all lands, seasons, and themes for his material, and may compel all forces to be the servants of his craft. Nevertheless his country lies near his heart, and in handling patriotic themes he chooses the open way and best. Of his perfect simplicity as a balladist the publishers seem to be aware. " Red Riding-Hood," " The Babes in the Wood," and " Putnam the Brave," composed at their suggestion, delighted young and old alike. In the present volume, " The Ballad of Valley Forge," " When this Old Flag was New," and that Parnassian counterpart to Eastman Johnson's glorious drawing, " The Little Drummer," show what genius can accomplish without striving after effect. We have the inspiration of the sibyl without the contortions. It looks easy, but try it! Nor can anything be better than " The Ballad of Crecy "—as healthy and surging as old Drayton's " Agincourt "—upon which, by the way, it is somewhat closely modelled.

Of the poems before us we are least attracted by the sentimental though finished studies from life which—

as a kind of sop to Cerberus, we suppose—are made to open the volume. They show less of the author's specific gift, though one—" After the Funeral "—is an exception, with an intense amount of genuine feeling crowded into its brief lyrical expression. We prefer to look further on to the works of graver purport, which give tone and character to the main body of the collection.

Stoddard's lyrics and madrigals, we have indicated, have the rare felicity of being spontaneous as a skylark's, and at the same time exquisite in delicacy of art. Two or three specimens will show that his voice has lost none of its sweetness:

> Wail on, thou bleeding nightingale!
>   I join my wail with thine;
> Deplore thy passion for the rose,
>   And let me weep for mine!
>
> Lament thy rose for seventy days,
>   She lives, and may reply;
> But mine is dead, and I must weep,
>   Or break my heart, and die!

THE DYING LOVER

> The grass that is under me now
>   Will soon be over me, sweet!
> When you walk this way again,
>   I shall not hear your feet.
>
> You may walk this way again,
>   And shed your tears like dew;
> They will be no more to me, then,
>   Than mine are now to you!

"I am a white falcon, hurrah!
  My home is the mountains so high;
But away o'er the lands and the waters,
  Wherever I please, I can fly.

"I wander from city to city,
  I dart from the wave to the cloud;
And when I am dead I shall slumber,
  With my own white wings for a shroud!"

———

"I know a little rose,
  And O but I were blest,
Could I but be the drop of dew
  That lies upon her breast!

"But I dare not look so high,
  Nor die a death so sweet;
It is enough for me to be
  The dust about her feet!"

The Horatian touch, that can add a grace to the
simplest theme, is visible in these dainty couplets:

TO A FRIEND, WITH A VASE

Poet, take this little vase,
From a lover of the race,
Given to hold—a funeral jar—
The ashes of thy loved cigar.
If for that it seem too fine,
Fill it to the brim with wine,
And drink, in love, to me and mine,
As I drain to thee and thine.
Ashes, though, may suit it best,
(There's a plenty in my breast);

[147]

Fill it, then, in summer hours
With the ashes of thy flowers—
Roses, such as on it blow,
Or lilies, like its ground of snow.

The English metrical period, with whose productions, so far as manner is concerned, Mr. Stoddard's
art now seems most in sympathy, is that of the Com-
monwealth and Restoration—the time of Wither,
Shirley, and Marvell, whose enduring metres he,
among contemporary poets, has made distinctively his
own, by infusing beneath their body a new and modern soul. In the pieces for which he chooses these
forms of expression, he rises above the Fancy which
lightens his songs, and Imagination—often sombre, but
sustained and noble—is their dominant force. The
gravity and stateliness of such measures are suited to
the themes for which he has selected them. There
is no better poetry in the book than that written in
honor of the great who have passed away, and of
one still among us. Certainly the piece entitled
" Abraham Lincoln: A Horatian Ode," is the finest
tribute yet paid to the memory of the Liberator. Its
monotone is grand throughout:

Not as when some great Captain falls
In battle, where his Country calls,
Beyond the struggling lines
That push his dread designs.
*   *   *   *
Nor as when sink the civic great,
The safer pillars of the State,
Whose calm, mature, wise words
Suppress the need of swords.

With no such tears as e'er were shed
  Above the noblest of our dead
Do we to-day deplore
The Man that is no more.

  Our sorrow hath a wider scope,
    Too strange for fear, too vast for hope,
A wonder, blind and dumb,
That waits—what is to come!

  Not more astounded had we been
    If Madness, that dark night, unseen,
Had in our chambers crept,
And murdered while we slept.

  We woke to find a mourning earth,
    Our Lares shivered on the hearth,
The roof-tree fallen, all
That could affright, appall!
          *   *   *   *
  O honest face, which all men knew!
    O tender heart, but known to few!
O wonder of the age,
Cut off by tragic rage!

To further illustrate the vigor of Mr. Stoddard's
imagination we will quote from another of this class
of poems. "Adsum," in commemoration of Thackeray, is widely known, and we pass it by. The opening of the ode written for Shakespeare's birthday is
very striking:

  She sat in her eternal home
    The sovereign mother of mankind;
Before her was the peopled world,
    The hollow night behind.

" Below my feet the thunders break,
    Above my head the stars rejoice;
But man, although he babbles much,
    Has never found a voice;

" Ten thousand years have come and gone,
    And not an hour of any day
But he has dumbly looked to me
    The things he could not say.

" It shall be so no more," she said;
    And then, revolving in her mind,
She thought, " I will create a child
    Shall speak for all his kind."

It was the spring-time of the year,
    And lo! where Avon's waters flow,
The child, her darling, came on earth,
    Three hundred years ago.

There was no portent in the sky,
    No cry, like Pan's, along the seas;
Nor hovered round his baby-mouth
    The swarm of classic bees.

"Vates Patriæ," which, if our memory serves us, was read at the Century Club on occasion of Mr. Bryant completing his 70th year, is remarkable for evenness and nobility of expression. It is as fine as Halleck's " Burns."

We are impressed by several poems of an elevated character, quite unlike anything before written, though involving no new methods of structure. They may be studied to advantage by people who confound orig-

inality with novel or grotesque rhythm. No one but
Stoddard could have written the solemn and mystical
" Invocation," or the Holbeinish " Catch " which fol-
lows it, and each is remarkable in its kind. " Rome "
and " Cæsar," companion pieces, are no less original in
conception and execution. But of all the poems one,
" Why Stand ye Gazing into Heaven? " is the most
impassioned and yet the most unsatisfying—the voice
not of an infant, but of an earnest, strong man

> ——crying in the night,
> And with no language but a cry!

It is the despair of the modern Lucretius. We
know too much and too little; have shaken off blind
superstition and fables new or old, and now stand
eager for some new revelation yet to come. The cry
comes from the depths of a resolute heart. When we
long to say to the poet, " Look upward," he makes
us feel that he is too self-pitiless to accept comfort
from that of which his reason knoweth not.

The solemnity of a large number of these poems is
very marked. They are not written in a minor key,
but are both profound and sad—the utterances of a
chastened spirit who has gone through the period at
which men like Clough strive to read the problem of
life, and is content to do his work and leave the rest
to that Power we do not comprehend. The tone to
which we refer may be distasteful to some, but there
are many readers even of modern poetry whose own
hearts sooner would lead them to the house of mourn-

ing than the house of joy. And nothing but affection for the poet can be awakened by the touching pathos of the lyrics in which he records his portion of the " one great Sorrow " which is " all over the wide, wide world." One can see that only the deepest wounds could yield such blood-red flowers of pain. In " The King's Sentinel " we also observe an exquisite passage which no one could have written but a father who had lost a darling child.

Mr. Stoddard's few poetical faults—neglect of synthetic structure, too great use of the parenthesis, occasional failure to simply express his thought—are rarely noticeable in this collection. And there are charming bits of sunshine, showing the natural lightness of the poet's heart, which flash in upon its pages here and there. Such is that wise and healthful poem, " The Country Life," from which our limits will not permit us to quote. We trust that the eminent publishers, to whom America has been indebted for admirable presentations of her foremost poets, will ere long give us in one compact volume the contents of this and Mr. Stoddard's earlier collections; nor can we refrain from expressing a hope that he himself will not suffer his devotion to those more exacting literary pursuits, in which he has a practical and scholarly eminence, to prevent his composition of some larger poetical work which shall be the measure and evidence of his full creative power.

In conclusion we reprint the grand Christmas Hymn, which will take its place as a standard portion of our choicest national song.

A CHRISTMAS HYMN TO AMERICA

Not as of old we keep the day
    Whereon the Prince of Peace was born,
Whose kingdom comes not!   Let us pray
    It comes this holy morn:
Let us begin it; make our brawlings cease,
And kill the hate that lurks behind the mask of Peace!

  Men of the South, if you recall
    The fields your valor won in vain,
Unchecked the manly tears may fall
    Above your heroes slain!
Weep! but remember we had heroes too,
As sadly dear to us as yours can be to you!

  Men of the North, whose sons and sires,
    Victorious in a hundred fights,
Gather no more about your fires
    In the long winter nights;
If some you loved are missing here and there,
No household at the South but mourns its vacant chair!

  By all the blood that has been shed,
    And will be till contentions cease,
Bury your anger with the dead,
    And be again at peace!
So, with your muskets rusting on the wall,
Your State shall be secure when greatest empires fall!

XI

MRS. STODDARD'S NOVELS [1]

ALL lovers of true literature will consider it both just and fortunate that Mrs. Stoddard's books of fiction should now be reproduced in standard library form, as a recognition of their place among works of fascinating interest and permanent value. These tales, their scenes and period, antedate the younger generation. Yet they are essentially modern, and in keeping with the choicest types of recent fiction. To be before one's time, in authorship, is as trying as to be born too late. If *The Morgesons, Two Men,* and *Temple House,* had not been written until the tempest of the Civil War was more fully assuaged, —if in other respects the season had been ripe,—they would have been received by the many, as they were by the critical few, for what they verily were—the pioneers of something new and real in the novelist's art.

—Of something real, without doubt, for the keynote of *Two Men* is surely that saying of Emerson's which precedes it: " Let us treat the men and women

[1] *A Critical Estimate of Mrs. Stoddard's Novels.* Introduction (revised version) to *TWO MEN.* Philadelphia: Henry T. Coates & Co., 1901.

MRS. STODDARD'S NOVELS

. . . as if they were real—perhaps they are." By the rule of her own nature, Mrs. Stoddard was among the first to break away from a prevailing false sentiment, to paint " things seen " as they are—to suggest the unseen as it must be.

But that her stories of human life, in a downeast village port, are " realistic," and were so in the adverse time of their first appearance, is not their vital claim. For they are " romantic," none the less, and often impassioned. I find little profit in the jealous conflict waged as to the values of the so-called realistic and romantic schools; save that it has brought out some good criticism, and that every such warfare is stimulating to both sides. Otherwise, it is chiefly an expression of one's taste or distaste for certain writers, or his opinion that too persistent fashions should in their turns give way. Often it is a dispute or confusion as to the meaning of a word. For who can doubt that art, to be of worth, must never be an abject copyist, yet should have its basis in life as it is and things as they are,—or that impassioned speech and action must be natural even in their intensity? Who does not feel that the most daring idealism must keep within the possibilities, as we conceive them, of nature; that Romance, with the bird of the Danish proverb, though soaring high, must seek its food on earth? Away then, like the author of these novels, from the mouthing, the stilted talk, the sentimentalism, of a pseudo-romantic school. On the other hand, of what value is a realistic work, with no strong personality behind it? The true question is—how much of invention, imagination, passion, has gone into its making? The method is nothing—nothing—compared with the quality of the practitioner. All methods, as time and fashion change, become the servants of genius: it does great things with all and in spite of any.

In these days of training and opportunity, moreover, there is a notion that most things can be effected by toil and culture; whereas, in all art, that which is significant is the result of a special gift—call it what you will. It comes with the uncommon touch, the sensitive ear and eye,—with that sixth sense, the vision which sees " what's under lock and key, man's soul." Mrs. Stoddard's novels appeal to us through a quality of their own. Written, I think, without much early practice, yet with experience of life, their strong original style—unmistakable as a human voice—is that of one with a gift, and the writer's instinct produces effects which a mere artist tries for in vain. Style, insight, originality, make books like *Two Men* and *Temple House* additions not merely to the bulk of reading, but to literature itself; as distinct in their kind as *Wuthering Heights* and *Margaret,* or even as *Père Goriot* or *Richard Feverel.* They express an individuality: many will like it, others may not, but it is here. The latter class must be blind, I think, to certain excellences. If we love nature, who sees its broad and minute features like this woman, or puts them in with more sure and brief touches,—rarely, and as a background to her groups and action, and through that innate knowledge of their subordinate use which belongs to the true dramatic faculty?

The human elements of *Two Men,* for example, seem the more notable for its narrow limits, and for the smallness of the stage on which tragedy and comedy are set forth. The personages are sharply outlined; their play of thought and passion is the more intense for an atmosphere of repression, the Puritan air, tempered by free ocean winds,—breathing which, many an Osmond Parke must needs be a rover and cosmopolite. Yet one is reminded of Thoreau's avowal that he knew the world, for he had travelled many years in Concord. Things and manners doubtless have changed in " Crest," but these folk are still modern— for we read their souls, and their speech bewrayeth them. Generations come and go in this short tale: its scenes of life, love and death are strangely impressive. The commonplace is here, but not dwelt upon, and slight actions are full of meaning; the bustle of Cuth and Elsa at their work, Jason's trick of throwing up his hammer and catching it on the turn,—these are characteristic and essential. How vividly, as the story goes on, each figure lives, moves, and has its being:—Sarah, the typical woman of her race, whose indomitable negative force keeps all within the circle of her narrow will—Cuth and Elsa, the family " help," faithful as dogs, reflecting and commenting like a Greek chorus—the winning, selfish, sensuous, irresolute Osmond and Parke—the wholesome and handsome Theresa—the noble Philippa, slow-moulded into perfect womanhood—the provincial village-folk—among all, over all, the grim form and visage of the heroic carpenter, Jason Auster, the downeast village Lincoln of our tale! *Les hommes sont rares,* and here is one to remember. Such a creation, of itself, lifts *Two Men* quite above the range of ordinary novels. The author's dramatic gift is illustrated by the picturesque and tragic episode of the quadroon mother and her daughters, the crime of Parke Auster, the fate of Charlotte—that beautiful, helpless, exotic flower of the tropics, blighted in the pitiless North.

Such a book will bear study. I have read it often, each time with a stronger perception of its author's individuality. Mrs. Stoddard's other novels, her short stories, her fugitive poems, are marked by the same qualities—they could be the work of no hand save her own. All seek to answer Parke Auster's question: " Such revelations come so unexpectedly from those who are the nearest to us! There is something appalling behind the screen of every-day life, countenance, custom, clothes. What is it?" Their faults, moreover, are characteristic. A few more readers, a quicker understanding of her work,—there being " something of summer even in the hum of insects "— would have stimulated her to the frequent labor which results in constructive perfection. Yet the wilding flavor of these early novels might have been lost in the process. Let us take them as they are, for so they are worth taking.

XII

MRS. STODDARD'S POEMS [1]

IN this highly characteristic book of Mrs. Stoddard's
verse we have the poetic harvest of a woman's
lifetime. Such a volume, coming from one whose
other work long since made its impression, has a significance which sets it apart from the books of verse
issued at successive intervals by even a justly favorite
poet. If not a disclosure, it is at least a confirmation,
of the author's personality. Readers of Mrs. Stoddard's novels and shorter tales have been aware of
the tense individuality which marks them. Her poetry
is the more direct expression of the same woman,
speaking with her own voice, and face to face, instead
of behind the masks of her personages. If, like a
holographic will, it were incumbent to prove it entirely
the writing of the devisor's hand, it would stand the
test. Here is plainly the author of *Two Men, The
Morgesons,* and *Temple House.* But to read her
verse is to get a new key to her prose. The often
evasive thought and circumstance of her fiction become
interpreted, like the Old World inscriptions read by
the aid of some bilingual tablet.

All in all, these are the poems of a reticent but most

[1] *New York Daily Tribune,* 1895.

[159]

original novelist, who at times has found prose inadequate for that self-expression which—in spite of theories as to the common ground of art—appears more essential, certainly more noble and welcome, in the case of a strong woman than in that of a strong man. Poems like "The Problem" and "In Memoriam" show us that thought, of itself, is often so subtle as to make speech rhythmical. But the rhythm of verse, if useful to thought, is almost indispensable to the more elevated states of feeling. Hence it is the glory and the charm of woman's verse that it is subjective, while a man's self-expression often drops into the weakness and effeminacy of the betrayed egotist.

Doubtless it is because in poetic language alone the most dynamic thought and feeling command a voice that the world cherishes many poets and tolerates yet more of them. The artistic unreality of verse enables the most reserved nature to reveal itself without being abashed. Among the writings of modern female poets, the eccentric half-formed lyrics of Emily Dickinson—a kind of intellectual diamond chips—were of interest chiefly for their quaint expression of unexpected thought. But as much as feeling is deeper than all thought, the verse of Mrs. Stoddard is truer poetry, not to speak of its saner intellectuality and purpose; to which elements the touch of art is added—of an art very decided in so various and pathetic a lyric as "Christmas Comes Again," but quite exceptional in the highest of metrical forms, that of her monodies in blank verse.

Mrs. Stoddard's sixty or seventy pieces, apparently

the selected verse of many years, are arranged so as
to show very well the modes and moods of work that
is the more effective for its compression within a limited range. The earlier division conveys its writer's
memories, and is imbued with that " pathetic fallacy "
which relates nature and even the decaying structures
of man to one's own feeling and experience. A melancholy bred of the passing away of kindred, and of
early associations, informs them. Their passion for
nature is strong and true; and this is quite in keeping
with the secret of " The House of Youth " and " The
House by the Sea." In these, and throughout Mrs.
Stoddard's verse, a thought is sometimes directly, but
not didactically, stated, and stays with the reader,
through an instinctive felicity of word or phrase. In
" The House of Youth " she says:

> The wind beats at the door,
> But never gets an answer back again,
> The silence is so proud;

and again,

> Man lives not in the past;
> None but a woman ever comes again
> Back to the " House of Youth."

Of November, she says:

> The naked, silent trees have taught me this—
> The loss of beauty is not always loss!

The last line has its corollary in a later reference
to autumn:

While watching in thy atmosphere, I see
The form of beauty changes, not its soul.

In the poem hereafter given, she speaks of nameless
plants, " perfect in their hues,"

Perfect in root and branch their plan of life,
As if the intention of a soul were there.

There are a few objective, and even dramatic, lyrics
in the middle of the volume—of which are " On the
Campagna," and the little pieces, full of sensuous melody and color, " A Midsummer Night " and " Mer-
cedes." These three, and " The Queen Deposed," have
rightly been culled by the anthologists, and show that
Mrs. Stoddard's lyrical quality, much less dominant
than her husband's—who was a lyrist from his youth
—is at times spontaneous and compulsive. " On the
Campagna," the lines on the tomb of Cecilia Metella,
is the most imaginative of the group—wrought in
an unrhymed measure, with a stately inscriptional effect, and as an objective study displaying the skill and
simple power that Matthew Arnold strove for and
twice or thrice attained. As to lighter strains, in a
vein affected by Owen Meredith, such as " A Few Idle
Words " and " Vers de Société," it cannot be said
that Mrs. Stoddard is fortunate. Her temperament
is too grave and deep, too genuinely moved, for the
work of a kind that market writers turn off deftly.

Where her power lies is, first, as has been intimated,
in her fusion of the spirit of nature—her familiar
wherever she has walked—with her own strength of

feeling; and, secondly, in the meditations of her blank verse, a measure which seems more adapted to her genius than that of any other woman of our time. Her handling of it is, in fact, unmistakable; it is but just to say that she is at her best in the stateliest, simplest and most difficult form of English verse. With its varied pauses, intervals and majestic cadence, it can be sustained only by the uplifting power of coefficient thought and diction. The slightest weakness at once betrays an incompetency. Nearly a score of these poems in blank verse, occupying a third of the volume, are of an even standard. The style is Mrs. Stoddard's own, differing from that of her husband—himself a master of the unrhymed pentameter —in the caesural method, and through its simpler limits of diction. The mental tone is fraught with the recognition of the mystery and transitoriness of things, but rises to content with a law that must be just and beneficent, because it is universal. A single poem of the series will show the pathos and beauty of her more impassioned utterance, and the discipline through which her genius has been matured.

UNRETURNING

Now all the flowers that ornament the grass,
Wherever meadows are and placid brooks,
Must fall—the " glory of the grass " must fall,
Year after year I see them sprout and spread—
The golden, glossy, tossing buttercups,
The tall, straight daisies and red clover globes,
The swinging bellwort and the blue-eyed bent,

[163]

With nameless plants as perfect in their hues—
Perfect in root and branch their plan of life,
As if the intention of a soul were there;
I see them flourish as I see them fall!

But he, who once was growing with the grass,
And blooming with the flowers, my little son,
Fell, withered—dead, nor has revived again!
Perfect and lovely, needful to my sight,
Why comes he not to ornament my days?
The barren fields forget that barrenness.

The soulless earth mates with these soulless things,
Why should I not obtain my recompense?
The budding spring should bring, or summer's prime,
At least a vision of the vanished child,
And let his heart commune with mine again,
Though in a dream—his life was but a dream;
Then might I wait with patient cheerfulness—
That cheerfulness which keeps one's tears unshed,
And blinds the eyes with pain—the passage slow
Of other seasons, and be still and cold
As the earth is when shrouded in the snow,
Or passive, like it, when the boughs are stripped
In autumn, and the leaves roll everywhere.

And he should go again; for winter's snows,
And autumn's melancholy voice, in winds,
In waters, and in woods, belong to me,
To me—a faded soul; for, as I said,
The sense of all his beauty, sweetness, comes
When blossoms are the sweetest; when the sea,
Sparkling and blue, cries to the sun in joy,
Or, silent, pale and misty waits the night,
Till the moon, pushing through the veiling cloud,
Hangs naked in its heaving solitude;
When feathery pines wave up and down the shore,

And the vast deep above holds gentle stars,
And the vast world beneath hides him from me!

" A Seaside Idyl," " The Chimney-Swallow's Idyl "
and " The Visitings of Truth" display Mrs. Stoddard's command of nature's themes. Her shorter
blank-verse poems have a quality kindred to that of
Emerson's " Days " and " The Snowstorm"; and of
her lyrics, the lines entitled " Why" might almost be
ascribed to the Concord sage. Two other poems, unrhymed—" As One " and " No Answer "—with idyllic
refrains, are successful in the isometric fashion of the
Syracusan eclogues, practised also by Tennyson in
the unrhymed songs of " The Princess " and the
" Idyls of the King."

The issue of this volume calls to mind the years in
which its author and her husband have lived and
worked together, wedded poets, whose respective utterances, far removed from interlikeness, are yet in
touching and absolute accord. Mrs. Stoddard's art,
to conclude, is that of one who, if she did not " lisp
in numbers," found the need of them in the joy and
sorrow of her womanhood, and has kept silent except
when moved by that stress of feeling which contents
itself with no petty or ignoble strain.

XIII

STODDARD'S LAST POEM [1]

THRENODY

Early or late, come when it will,
   At midnight or at noon,
Promise of good, or threat of ill,
   Death always comes too soon.
To the child who is too young to know,
   (Pray heaven he never may!)
   This life of ours is more than play,—
A debt contracted long ago
   Which he perforce must pay;
   And the man whose head is gray,
And sad, is fain to borrow,
Albeit with added pain and sorrow,
   The comfort of delay;
   Only let him live to-day—
There will be time to die to-morrow!
Now there is not an hour to spare,
   Under the uncertain sky,
Save to pluck roses for the hair
Of the loving and the fair,
And the kisses following these,
Like a swarming hive of bees
   That soar on high,
Till, drunken with their own sweet wine,
   They fall and die.

[1] *Putnam's Monthly and The Critic,* October, 1906.

When dear words have all been said
   And bright eyes no longer shine
   (Ah, not thine!)
   Close these weary eyes of mine,
And bear me to the lonely bed
   Where unhonored I shall lie,
   While the tardy years go by,
   Without question or reply
From the long-forgotten dead.

THIS threnody proved to be the swan-song of its
author—of the old minstrel who in his spring-
time had made the early volumes of this magazine
tuneful with a unique succession of ballads, songs, and
graver poems. If, as Shelley says, " We begin in what
we end," it is fitting that this poem, his wife's requiem
and his own, should be enshrined in the first new
number of a periodical in which his gift attained maturity and secured for him, notwithstanding the old-
time rule of anonymity, a repute that justified his
adoption of authorship as a profession.

The lyric now printed for the first time was the
only one perfected from many broken cadences which
came to him in the final year of his life. It was composed while his wife, Elizabeth Stoddard (older than
himself), was plainly nearing her end. She died in
her eightieth year, August 1, 1902: the eleventh day
after the date affixed to the poem. Eleven months
before, the wedded poets had lost their only son,
Lorimer—author of poems, pictures, and successful
dramas,—and Mr. Stoddard had borne up under the
affliction less stoically than his wife; for a time seeming dazed, and having illusions that were intensified

by his blindness and partial paralysis. During Mrs. Stoddard's fatal illness, his brain teemed with images and melodies which he could not get into form. The snatches of song, nevertheless, which were taken down imperfectly by his attendant, were quite as coherent as the thumb-nail sketches of an artist, or the first notes of a writer, and if the poet could have renewed his power of work but for an interval, beautiful results might have come from them.

As it was, under stress of an unusual excitement he ever had but one refuge—that of artistic expression. From an almost illegible note to me, dated, but not then delivered, " Sept. 3, 1902, *circa* 10:30," I can make out such bits as these: " I have done in the rough, since say July 6, some twenty or more poems, possibly . . . some good others bad. . . . But, no indeed, I think I have been an instrument with which unseen hands played their own tunes. I never made these things. . . . would be glad if I could. Puck and Ober have let loose in 15th Street, Liberty and Sag Harbor, and the pipers have been paid." One of these poems was this threnody, which seems to reveal an intensely poetic renascence of the lyrical quality and thought of a noble prime—which so few now living can recall to mind. Few indeed survive who knew him before the maladies which came upon him in middle age so told upon his spirits and bodily power. The lyric is given exactly according to a version which Mr. Stoddard managed to write for me with his own hand, except for some needful punctuation and indentation. I have · resisted advice to separate its three natural strophes or divisions, feeling that his instinct was true in making it a continuous strain.

Of all poets of his time, Stoddard had most dwelt upon death,—striking its whole gamut, and not confining his song to the one topic which Poe declared to be above all "the most poetical in the world." Within the year his gifted and only surviving son had died in the hour of best achievement; his life-long companion, the one woman he had loved, was hastening to the grave; he confronted desolation, which could find "surcease" only through his own impending journey to "the hollow vale." The opening quatrain of the requiem is the sole verse which I recall that declares, with the compressed force of sternly simple diction, that at every age—even in extreme old age—"Death always comes too soon." The four lines are strong enough to carry the whole poem, and the eleven which follow do not lessen their effect. In the second division, commencing with "Now there is not an hour to spare," there is a poignant and momentary loss of hold; the poet's ear and fancy are lured by his own melody; his grief is lulled by vague yet exquisite wanderings of song. Then, recovering as if from a trance, he is brought back to his desolation, to acceptance of the irreparable and to a sense of his own approaching end. He strikes the key of hopeless resignation, and from the line "When dear words have all been said" to the close maintains it, albeit with an old man's mingling echoes of the measures which most affected him in youth. In fine, the

opening division of this sweet, sad monody was un-
mistakably his own—that of the man who always
faced openly, but without appeal, a relentless fate or
situation. None but himself could have written this
lyric; as a whole its effect is synthetic, and indisputa-
bly that of his swan-song—not of a kind with Tennyson's " Crossing the Bar," or with the " Prospice "
and " Epilogue " of Browning, but charged with the
" ruling passion " of a poet who half a century before
had sung:

> There is but one great sorrow
> All over the wide, wide world.

Putnam's Monthly, from the first, welcomed the
young New York poet, and Stoddard well repaid its
hospitality. He had previously, it is true, written
much verse; had published and suppressed a booklet,
and then made up a volume of poems full of promise,
with open indebtedness to Keats, the idol of his formative period—as Shelley was of Bayard Taylor's. His
contributions to the *Monthly,* however, were soon rec-
ognizable through a fresh and individual tone which
was peculiar to his unstudied songs and sustained
pieces, if not to his enforced journey work, through
his after career. The series, which extended from
March, 1853, to the number for November, 1856,—
the last issue but one of the magazine,—embraced a
full score of poems; so many and so good as to constitute their author, one may say, the laureate, certainly the chief minnesinger, of that eminently American periodical. Doubtless some of his songs were the

more available for their brevity, but they also had the true *lieder* quality, the modern scarcity of which is now checking a custom of filling half-pages with the stanzas and sonnets at command. The poems, short and long, accepted from Stoddard by the *Putnam* editors appear to outnumber those of all the other contributors, and to hold their own in choice companionship. For it was in *Putnam's* that Longfellow's "Two Angels," "The Warden of the Cinque Ports," "The Jewish Cemetery at Newport," and that most haunting of his lyrics, "My Lost Youth," first appeared, not to mention three minor pieces. Bryant contributed his "Robert of Lincoln," and Lowell at least four characteristic poems; Bayard Taylor as many, equally good; Mrs. Stoddard, one of her earliest lyrics. I must not forget to mention the picturesque verse of Rose Terry, or the poems of a quaint singer, E. W. Ellsworth, which made us impatient of his reticence in after years. Aldrich probably was the youngest of all those who had the pleasure of seeing their measures on the fair pages of the *Monthly;* in his "Legend of Elsinore" can be found the dawning charm of his maturer genius and more fastidious art. Meanwhile a country boy, still under age, was surprised when certain stanzas entitled "Amavi," which he had mailed to *Putnam's* at a venture, were printed there in October, 1853, and was glad of the check earned by his first offer of a poem to any magazine. He still remembers just as vividly the delight given by Stoddard's lyrics, from the date of the appearance of a tiny avatar of the new mode—the little poem "At

Rest," which made him eagerly read subsequent offer-
ings by the same unmistakable hand. Among these
were " The Shadow," and the most often quoted of the
poet's shorter madrigals, " There are gains for all our
losses," which bore in *Putnam's* the title of "Night
and Morning." Its author's work culminated in Vol.
VIII, 1856, with " The Fisher and Charon," a veritable masterpiece of blank-verse, to which many pages
were not begrudged. I would ask any young writer
to go back to this heroic idyl, and regard its human
pathos, its calm imaginative progress, its stately diction, and mark what a structure its maker,—just escaped from apprenticeship in an iron-foundry,—built
upon the stray text of a minor classic, infusing it, by
intuition as sure as that of Keats, with the very soul
of the antique. If this had been the handiwork of
the author of " Sohrab and Rustum " and " Emped-
ocles on Etna," or of Lowell—who had essayed the
theme of " Rhœcus," undaunted by the finer classicism
of Landor's " Hamadryad,"—it would have vastly impressed the down-east Areopagus to whose verdict
alone (as Poe often complained) much deference was
shown at that stage of our æsthetic development.

As it was, Ticknor and Fields in 1857 brought out
an alluring volume, *Songs of Summer,* containing
the whole series of Stoddard's *Putnam* contributions
and thrice their number of additional poems. This
collection, with Taylor's *Songs of the Orient,* Aldrich's new volumes, and the poems of others af-
filiated by instinct or association, were fresh with the
ardor of a new clan, devoted to poetry for its own

sake, to art and beauty and feeling; and this in no spirit of preciosity, but as a departure from—though not a revolt against—the moralizing and reformatory propaganda, howsoever great in purpose and achievement, of the venerated " elder bards."

XIV

AUSTIN DOBSON [1]

AN usher at the drawing-room door serves as a foil to the courtly groups beyond him. All his bows and flourishes seem commonplace beside the easy grace of his betters, if, indeed, the guests vouchsafe him a glance as they pass within. Little they care whether his legs be cross-gartered. Still, the usher is thought to be, in his way, a useful personage. And an introduction to these Vignettes in Rhyme thus may bear a certain fitness,—lest otherwise the collection should lack that effect which some prosaic contrast may lend to the delicate art of the whole.

Once acquainted with these pages, the reader will find that my comparison is an apt one; that he is in good company, and that Mr. Dobson, more than other recent poets, seems not only to gather about him a select concourse of fine people, but to move at ease among them. It is a pleasure to meet these gentlefolk, and like a mark of our own rank. Here are gathered, it is true, those of various periods and manners, but all demean themselves with graceful breeding and without affectation, and are on good terms with one another and with their host. Here are the old noblesse,

[1] Introduction to *Vignettes in Rhyme, and Other Verses.* New York: Henry Holt & Company, 1880.

[174]

the *beau sabreur,* the gentleman and gentlewoman of the old school, and here the youths and maidens of to-day,—a choice assemblage, with not a prig, a bore, or a vulgarian among them.

Some of the most attractive portions of this selection, therefore, have to do with the quaint people of a time gone by, and with the treasures they have bequeathed to us. But the author is an artist of the present, and his work a product of to-day. Its modernism is a constant charm. There are in England and France so many lovely relics of a refined, alluring age! In England, the canvases of Sir Joshua and Gainsborough, the old houses with their souvenirs of teacup-times,—brocade and chintz, deftly garnished mantels, tapestried and lavendered chambers, box-bordered lawns and garden-plots. In France, the dark hangings and polished floors of stately mirrored rooms in turreted châteaux and peaked mansions. Never so much as now have the artists availed themselves of these materials, and of the riches of galleries and museums close at hand. But one looks to the poet to catch the sense and soul of these things, the aroma that clings about them. The fashions that most readily appeal to Mr. Dobson are those which are so far bygone as to be again desired and new. What more odious than the mode we have just discarded? What so winning as that of a time earlier than our memory, and thoroughly good in its time? The movement which has given expression to all this, on both sides of the ocean, is like a new taste. Mr. Dobson is the instinctive and born interpreter of its sentiment, and

[175]

his *Vignettes in Rhyme* will be as welcome to us as they have been to his own people. The actor's art delights us, because we know it is not real, and the modern renaissance delights us, because it gives us something quite apart from our common humdrum life; it is a feeling of to-day that dallies with the fragments of the past,—of that Past which never is past, which merges with the Present, and retains a hold upon our works of every-day use and beauty.

I write first of Mr. Dobson's old-time sentiment, because it is so definite and effective, but his muse is not restricted to a single range. Before looking farther, let us see who is this artist that has filled the vacant niche, and whose verse shows at once the strength and fineness that make it rank with the selectest poetry of our day.

Not unlike others who live at will in an ideal world, Austin Dobson is as modest and unassuming a person as one often meets. Just a poet, scholar and gentleman, the artist-side of whose nature compensates him for any lack of adventure in his daily work and walk. As is the case with many London authors, an office in the Civil Service has supplied him with an honorable certainty of livelihood and left his heart at ease for song. He was born in 1840, and has been a government-clerk for twenty-two years. Singularly enough, he did not begin to write poetry till he was twenty-five years of age, and the first collection of his *Vignettes* was not made until 1874. From the outset he took the public taste with the delicate sense and humor of his lyrics, no less than by their finish and ideality. We reasonably may surmise that years of growth, study, observation, lay behind this good fortune.

My own attention, I remember, first was drawn to his work by the neatest and brightest of society-verse, composed in a novel style, quite unlike that of Praed, Locker, or his earlier predecessors. I have elsewhere described poems of this class as " those patrician rhymes, which, for want of an English equivalent, are termed *vers de société*. . . . This is pervaded by an indefinable grace that elevates it to the region of poetic art, and owing to which the lightest ballads of Suckling and Waller are current to this day. In fine, the true kind is marked by humor, by spontaneity, joined with extreme elegance of finish, by the quality we call breeding,—above all, by lightness of touch." All of these essentials were present in " Tu Quoque," " An Autumn Idyll," and in other pieces which at once brought Mr. Dobson into favor. Some of them are so witty and elegant, surrounded by so fine an atmosphere, and withal so true to the feeling and scenery of his own island, as to make him seem like a modern Horace or Theocritus, or like both in one. He is not the first poet that has been called an English Horace, but few have better merited the title. He draws his Englishmen as Horace drew his town and country friends. It seems to me that he is the sketcher to whom Thackeray would take a liking. Since the De Floracs, we have had no such French people as L'Etoile and Monsieur Vieuxbois; since Esmond and his times, no such people of the old England have

come to life again as Mr. Dobson's " Gentleman "
and " Gentlewoman," his " Dorothy," or even that
knight of the road, whose untimely taking-off is re-
hearsed in " The Ballad of ' Beau Brocade.' "

Our debonair poet elevates taste and feeling to the
pitch of imagination. He yields himself to the spell
of brooding memories and associations:

> We shut our hearts up, now-a-days,
> Like some old music-box that plays
> Unfashionable airs that raise
>   Derisive pity;
> Alas,—a nothing starts the spring:
> And lo, the sentimental thing
> At once commences, quavering
>   Its lover's ditty.

His pathos and tenderness appear, too, in more serious
pieces. There are kind touches in " The Child-Mu-
sician," " The Cradle," and " A Nightingale in
Kensington Gardens." Mr. Brander Matthews, one
of our own most agreeable writers, justly lays stress
upon Dobson's perfect absorption in his immediate
theme, his art of shutting out from a poem everything
foreign to its needs. How purely Greek the image
of Autonoë! How minute the picture of " An Old
Fish-Pond," and what shrewd wisdom! What human
nature in " A Dead Letter," one of my favorite pieces,
—and how perfect its reproduction of the ancestral
mode! With all his regard for " values," the poet
never goes to the pseudo-æsthetic extreme; indeed, he
is the first to poke fun at it, and seems quite free from
certain affectations of modern verse. His English is

pure and simple, and the natural finish of his poetry shows for itself. I doubt if there is another collection of lyrics by an English singer more devoid of blemishes, more difficult to amend by the striking-out or change of words and measures. Mr. Aldrich has suggested that it may well be compared, in this respect, to the French of such an artist as Théophile Gautier, —the lesson of whose L'Art, as will be seen from his own crystalline poem in imitation, Mr. Dobson long ago took to heart.

His lyrical studies and dialogues upon French themes of the Eighteenth Century are full of poetic realism. In " Une Marquise," and in " The Story of Rosina,"—a sustained piece which shows the higher range of its author's genius,—the presiding beauty, and the artist of a time and a region

> Wherein most things went naked, save the Truth,

are made known to us more truly than they dared to know themselves. For dainty workmanship, and comprehension of the spirit of an age, read " The Metamorphosis," and its sequel, " The Song out of Season." What other poet could have written these, or " Good-night, Babette!"—which contains the Angelus song, whose loveliness I scarcely realized until Mr. Aldrich printed it by itself, a gem taken from its setting. And I know not, since reading " The Curé's Progress," where else to find so attractive an ideal of the goodness, quaintness, sweetness, of the typical *Père* on his journey down the street of his little town. The town itself is depicted, in a few stanzas, as plainly as

[179]

"Our Village" in the whole series of Miss Mitford's classic sketches.

Mr. Dobson escapes the restrictions of many writers of elegant verse by his refreshing variety. In his lightest work he is a fine poet at play; not a weakling, with one pretty gift, doing the best thing in his power. He is entitled to the credit, whatever that may be, of having been among the first to really bring into fashion the present use of old French stanzaic and rhythmic forms. In view of the speed wherewith these have been adopted and played upon by poets and parodists without number, I am not sure whether to thank him or to condole with him. We must acknowledge that English poetry, like the language, is eclectic, deriving its riches from many sources. Its lyrical score, which long has been too monotonous, doubtless will gain something from the revival of these continental forms. Only those suited to the genius of our song will come into permanent use. If any readers are as yet unacquainted with the nature and varieties of these old-new forms, they can find the best exposition of them in Mr. Edmund Gosse's "Plea for Certain Exotic Forms of Verse." [1] The specimens of the Rondel, the Rondeau, the Triolet, the Villanelle, the Ballade, the Chant Royal, which he cites from the works of Swinburne, Lang, Dobson, and those of his own sweet and learned muse, are excellently done. Nearer home, we have Mr. Matthews's analysis [2] of Mr. Dobson's experiments in all these forms of verse,

[1] *Cornhill Magazine*, July, 1877.
[2] *Appleton's Journal*, June, 1878.

and a farther description on my part is rendered unnecessary.

Most of the poems of this class in the following pages first were brought together systematically in Dobson's *Proverbs in Porcelain,* 1877, although all of their modes, except the Chant Royal and the Villanelle, can be found in the relics of early English poetry,—some even in the verse of Gower and Chaucer. My own creed is that the chief question is not what novelty tempts us to the show, but whether the show be a good one,—and Mr. Dobson pleasantly avows a kindred belief. Some of these exotic forms seem to be handled as cleverly by him in English, as in French by De Banville. The *villanelle* " For a Copy of Theocritus," is like a necklace of beaten antique gold. His *rondeaux* " To Ethel " and " When *Finis* Comes," have a tricksy spirit, a winged and subtle perfection. Their rules seem peculiarly suited to experiments in translation from Horace. At all events, I do not recall any paraphrases of " O Fons Bandusiæ " and " Vixi Puellis " more satisfactory in form and flavor than those which Mr. Dobson gives us.

Reviewing these *Vignettes in Rhyme* and *Proverbs in Porcelain,* I have felt like one who has the freedom of a virtuoso's collection,—who handles unique and precious things, fearing that his clumsiness may leave a blemish or in some way cost him dear. Artist and poet at once, Mr. Dobson reminds me of Francia, who " loved to sign his paintings ' Aurifex,' and on his trinkets inscribed the word ' Pictor,'" and I have an impression that rarely of late has an English

singer offered us more charming portraits, purer
touches of nature, more picturesque glimpses of a
manor which he holds in fee. It is hard to define his
limitations, for he has not yet gone beyond them; yet
I shall not be surprised if his future career shall prove
them to be outside the " liberties " which even a
friendly critic might assign to him.

XV

EUGENE FIELD

"ALAS, POOR YORICK!"[1]

IN paying a tribute to the mingled mirth and tenderness of Eugene Field—the poet of whose going
the West may say, " He took our daylight with him "
—one of his fellow journalists has written that he was
a jester, but not of the kind that Shakespeare drew
in Yorick. He was not only,—so the writer implied,
—the maker of jibes and fantastic devices, but the
bard of friendship and affection, of melodious lyrical
conceits; he was the laureate of children—dear for his
"Wynken, Blynken and Nod" and "Little Boy
Blue"; the scholarly book-lover, withal, who relished
and paraphrased his Horace, who wrote with delight
a quaint archaic English of his special devising; who
collected rare books, and brought out his own *Little
Books* of *Western Verse* and *Profitable Tales* in
high-priced limited editions, with broad margins of
paper that moths and rust do not corrupt, but which
tempts bibliomaniacs to break through and steal.

[1] Introduction to *The Holy Cross, and Other Tales*. New
York: Charles Scribner's Sons, 1901. [Originally contributed to
the *Souvenir Book* of the New York Hebrew Fair, December,
1895.]

For my own part, I would select Yorick as the very forecast, in imaginative literature, of our various Eugene. Surely Shakespeare conceived the " mad rogue " of Elsinore as made up of grave and gay, of wit and gentleness, and not as a mere clown or " jig maker." It is true that when Field put on his cap and bells, he too was " wont to set the table on a roar," as the feasters at a hundred tables, from " Casey's Table d'Hôte " to the banquets of the opulent East, now rise to testify. But Shakespeare plainly reveals, concerning Yorick, that mirth was not his sole attribute,— that his motley covered the sweetest nature and the tenderest heart. It could be no otherwise with one who loved and comprehended childhood and whom the children loved. And what does Hamlet say?— " He hath borne me upon his back a thousand times . . . Here hung those lips that I have kissed I know not how oft! " Of what is he thinking but of his boyhood, before doubts and contemplation wrapped him in the shadow, and when in his young grief or frolic the gentle Yorick, with his jest, his " excellent fancy," and his songs and gambols, was his comrade?

Of all moderns, then, here or in the old world, Eugene Field seems to be most like the survival, or revival, of the ideal jester of knightly times; as if Yorick himself were incarnated, or as if a superior bearer of the bauble at the court of Italy, or of France, or of English King Hal, had come to life again—as much out of time as Twain's Yankee at the Court of Arthur; but not out of place,—for he fitted himself as aptly to his folk and region as Puck to the

fays and mortals of a wood near Athens. In the days
of divine sovereignty, the jester, we see, was by all
odds the wise man of the palace; the real fools were
those he made his butt—the foppish pages, the obsequi-
ous courtiers, the swaggering guardsmen, the insolent
nobles, and not seldom majesty itself. And thus it is
that painters and romancers have loved to draw him.
Who would not rather be Yorick than Osric, or Touch-
stone than Le Beau, or even poor Bertuccio than one
of his brutal mockers? Was not the redoubtable
Chicot, with his sword and brains, the true ruler of
France? To come to the jesters of history—which is
so much less real than fiction—what laurels are greener
than those of Triboulet, and Will Somers, and John
Heywood—dramatist and master of the king's merry
Interludes? Their shafts were feathered with mirth
and song, but pointed with wisdom, and well might
old John Trussell say "That it often happens that
wise counsel is more sweetly followed when it is tempered with folly, and earnest is the less offensive if it be
delivered in jest."

Yes, Field "caught on" to his time—a complex
American, with the obstreperous *bizarrerie* of the frontier and the artistic delicacy of our oldest culture
always at odds within him—but he was, above all,
a child of nature, a frolic incarnate, and just as he
would have been in any time or country. Fortune had
given him that unforgettable mummer's face,—that
clean-cut, mobile visage,—that animated natural
mask! No one else had so deep and rich a voice for
the rendering of the music and pathos of a poet's lines,

and no actor ever managed both face and voice better than he in delivering his own verses merry or sad. One night, he was seen among the audience at " Uncut Leaves," and was instantly requested to do something towards the evening's entertainment. As he was not in evening dress, he refused to take the platform, but stood up in the lank length of an ulster, from his corner seat, and recited "Dibdin's Ghost" and "Two Opinions" in a manner which blighted the chances of the readers that came after him. It is true that no clown ever equalled the number and lawlessness of his practical jokes. Above all, every friend that he had —except the Dean of his profession, for whom he did exhibit unbounded and filial reverence—was soon or late a victim of his whimsicality, or else justly distrusted the measure of Field's regard for him. Nor was the friendship perfected until one bestirred himself to pay Eugene back in kind. As to this, I am only one of scores now speaking from personal experience. There seemed to be no doubt in his mind that the victim of his fun, even when it outraged common sensibilities, *must* enjoy it as much as he. Who but Eugene, after being the welcome guest, at a European capital, of one of our most ambitious and refined ambassadors, would have written a lyric, sounding the praises of a German "onion pie," ending each stanza with

Ach, Liebe! Ach, mein Gott!

and would have printed it in America, with his host's initials affixed?

My own matriculation at Eugene's College of Unreason was in this wise. In 1887, Mr. Ben Ticknor, the Boston publisher, was complaining that he needed some new and promising authors to enlarge his booklist. The New York *Sun* and *Tribune* had been copying Field's rhymes and prose extravaganzas—the former often very charming, the latter the broadest satire of Chicago life and people. I suggested to Mr. Ticknor that he should ask the poet-humorist to collect, for publication in book-form, the choicest of his writings thus far. To make the story brief, Mr. Field did so, and the outcome—at which I was somewhat taken aback—was the remarkable book, *Culture's Garland,* with its title imitated from the sentimental " Annuals " of long ago, and its cover ornamented with sausages linked together as a coronal wreath! The symbol certainly fitted the greater part of the contents, which ludicrously scored the Chicago " culture " of that time, and made Pullman, Armour, and other commercial magnates of the Lakeside City special types in illustration. All this had its use, and many of the sufferers long since became the *farceur's* devoted friends. The Fair showed the country what Chicago really was and is. Certainly there is no other American city where the richest class appear so enthusiastic with respect to art and literature. " The practise of virtue makes men virtuous," and even if there was some pretence and affectation in the culture of ten years ago, it has resulted in as high standards of taste as can elsewhere be found. Moreover, if our own " four hundred " had even affected, or made it the fashion to be interested in, whatever makes for real culture, the intellectual life of this metropolis would not now be so far apart from the " social swim." There were scattered through *Culture's Garland* not a few of Field's delicate bits of verse. In some way he found that I had instigated Mr. Ticknor's request, and, although I was thinking solely of the publisher's interests, he expressed unstinted gratitude. Soon afterwards I was delighted to receive from him a quarto parchment " breviary," containing a dozen ballads, long and short, engrossed in his exquisitely fine handwriting, and illuminated with colored borders and drawings by the poet himself. It must have required days for the mechanical execution, and certainly I would not now exchange it for its weight in diamonds. This was the way our friendship began. It was soon strengthened by meetings and correspondence, and never afterwards broken.

Some years ago, however, I visited Chicago, to lecture, at the invitation of its famous social and literary " Twentieth Century Club." This was Eugene's opportunity, and I ought not to have been as dumfounded as I was, one day, when our evening papers copied from the *Chicago Record* a " very pleasant joke " at the expense of his town and myself! It was headed: " Chicago Excited! Tremendous Preparations for His Reception," and went on to give the order and route of a procession that was to be formed at the Chicago station and escort me to my quarters—stopping at Armour's packing-yards and the art-galleries on the way. It included the " Twentieth Century

Club" in carriages, the "Browning Club" in busses, and the "Homer Club" in drays; ten millionaire publishers, and as many pork-packers, in a chariot drawn by white horses, followed by not less than two hundred Chicago poets afoot! I have no doubt that Eugene thought I would enjoy this kind of advertisement as heartily as he did. If so, he lacked the gift of putting himself in the other man's place. But his sardonic face, a-grin like a school-boy's, was one with two others which shone upon me when I did reach Chicago, and my pride was not wounded sufficiently to prevent me from enjoying the restaurant luncheon to which he bore me off in triumph. I did promise to square accounts with him, in time, and this is how I fulfilled my word. The next year, at a meeting of a suburban "Society of Authors," a certain lady journalist was chaffed as to her acquaintanceship with Field, and accused of addressing him as "Gene." At this she took umbrage, saying: "It's true we worked together on the same paper for five years, but he was always a perfect gentleman. I *never* called him 'Gene.'" This was reported by the press, and gave me the refrain for a skit entitled "Katharine and Eugenio":

> Five years she sate a-near him
>   Within that type-strewn loft;
> She handed him the paste-pot,
>   He passed the scissors oft;
> They dipped in the same inkstand
>   That crowned their desk between,
> Yet—he never called her Katie,
>   She never called him "Gene".

Though close—ah! close—the droplight
  That classic head revealed,
She was to him Miss Katharine,
  He—naught but Mister Field;
Decorum graced his upright brow
  And thinned his lips serene,
And, though he wrote a poem each hour,
  Why should she call him " Gene "?

She gazed at his sporadic hair—
  She knew his hymns by rote;
They longed to dine together
  At Casey's table d'hôte;
Alas, that Fortune's " hostages "—
  But let us draw a screen!
He dared not call her Katie;
  How *could* she call him " Gene "?

I signed my verses " By one of Gene's Victims "; they appeared in *The Tribune,* and soon were copied by papers in every part of the country. Other stanzas, with the same refrain, were added by the funny men of the Southern and Western press, and it was months before " Gene " saw the last of them. The word " Eugenio," which was the name by which I always addressed him in our correspondence, left him in no doubt as to the initiator of the series, and so our " Merry War " ended, I think, with a fair quittance to either side.

Grieving, with so many others, over Yorick's premature death, it is a solace for me to remember how pleasant was our last interchange of written words. Not long ago, he was laid very low by pneumonia, but recovered, and before leaving his sick-room wrote me a sweetly serious letter—with here and there a sparkle in it—but in a tone sobered by illness, and full of yearning for a closer companionship with his friends. At the same time he sent me the first editions, long ago picked up, of all my earlier books, and begged me to write on their fly-leaves. This I did; with pains to gratify him as much as possible, and in one of the volumes wrote this little quatrain:

TO EUGENE FIELD

Death thought to claim you in this year of years,
    But Fancy cried—and raised her shield between—
" Still let men weep, and smile amid their tears;
    Take any two beside, but spare Eugene! "

In view of his near escape, the hyperbole, if such there was, might well be pardoned, and it touched Eugene so manifestly that—now that the eddy indeed has swept him away, and the Sabine Farm mourns for its new-world Horace—I cannot be too thankful that such was my last message to him.

Eugene Field was so mixed a compound that it will always be impossible quite to decide whether he was wont to judge critically of either his own conduct or his literary creations. As to the latter, he put the worst and the best side by side, and apparently cared alike for both. That he did much beneath his standard, fine and true at times,—is unquestionable, and many a set of verses went the rounds that harmed his reputation. On the whole, I think this was due to the fact that he got his stated income as a newspaper poet and jester, and had to furnish his score of

" Sharps and Flats " with more or less regularity. For all this, he certainly has left pieces, compact of the rarer elements, sufficient in number to preserve for him a unique place among America's most original characters, scholarly wits, and poets of brightest fancy. Yorick is no more! But his genius will need no chance upturning of his grave-turf for its remembrance. When all is sifted, its fame is more likely to strengthen than to decline.

XVI

EDWIN BOOTH[1]

WHEN we mark the struggles of a brave spirit
against the restrictions of an ignoble body,
we pay admiring honors to every success that it
achieves. It is the contest between human will and
untoward fate. Each triumph is a victory of man's
dearest heritage, spiritual power. Some have made
themselves great captains despite physical weakness
and natural fear; scholars and writers have become
renowned, though slow to learn, or, haply, " with wisdom at one entrance quite shut out "; nor have stam-
mering lips and shambling figure prevented the rise
of orators and actors, determined to give utterance to
the power within. But, in our approval of the energy
that can so vanquish the injuries of fortune, we are
apt to overrate its quality, and to forget how much
more exquisite the endowment would be if allied with
those outward resources which complete the full
largess of Heaven's favoritism. In the latter case we
yield our unqualified affection to beings who afford
us an unqualified delight. We are reverencing the
gifts of the gods; and in their display see clearly that
no human will can secure that nobility of appearance

[1] *The Atlantic Monthly,* May, 1866.

and expression which a few maintain without intention, and by right of birth.

Bodily fitness is no small portion of a genius for any given pursuit; and, in the conduct of life, the advantages of external beauty can hardly be overrated. All thinkers have felt this. Emerson says " of that beauty which reaches its perfection in the human form," that " all men are its lovers; wherever it goes, it creates joy and hilarity, and everything is permitted to it." Now there is a beauty of parts, which is external; and another of the expression of the soul, which is the superior. But in its higher grades the former implies the latter. Socrates said that his ugliness accused just as much in his soul, had he not corrected it by education. And Montaigne writes: " The same word in Greek signifies both fair and good, and Holy Word often calls those good which it would call fair "; and, moreover, " Not only in the men that serve me, but also in the beasts, I consider this point within two finger-breadths of goodness."

Can we claim too much for physical adaptation in our measure of the rank to be accorded an actor? For he of all others, not excepting the orator, makes the most direct personal appeal to our tastes. In his own figure he holds the mirror up to Nature, while his voice must be the echo of her various tones. By the law of aristocracy in art, he must be held so much the greater, as he is able to depict the nobler manifestations of her forms and passions. Of course the first excellence is that of truth. A spirited enactment of Malvolio, of Falstaff, or of Richard Crookback has the high merit of faithfully setting forth humanity, though in certain whimsical or distorted phases; but we are more profoundly enriched by the portrayal of higher types. And thus, in making an actor's chosen and successful studies a means of measuring his genius, we find in the self-poise which wins without effort, and must throughout sustain the princely Hamlet, or Othello tender and strong, that grand manner which, in painting, places the art of Raphael and Angelo above that of Hogarth or Teniers. Each may be perfect in its kind, but one kind exceeds another in glory.

We have two pictures before us. One, on paper yellow with the moth of years, is the portrait of an actor in the costume of Richard III. What a classic face! English features are rarely cast in that antique mould. The head sits lightly on its columnar neck, and is topped with dark-brown curls, that cluster like the acanthus; the gray eyes are those which were justly described as being "at times full of fire, intelligence, and splendor, and again of most fascinating softness"; and the nose is of "that peculiar Oriental construction, which gives an air of so much distinction and command." Such was the countenance of Junius Brutus Booth,—that wonderful actor, who, to powers of scorn, fury, and pathos rivalling those which illumined the uneven performances of Edmund Kean, added scholastic attainments which should have equalized his efforts, and made every conception harmonious with the graces of a philosophical and cultured soul. In structure the genius of the elder Booth was indeed closely akin to that of Kean, if not the rarer of the two, notwithstanding the triumphant assertion of Doran, who says that Booth was driven by Kean's superiority to become a hero to "transpontine audiences." Each relied upon his intuitive, off-hand conception of a given part, and fell back to nature in his methods, throwing aside conventionalisms which had long ruled the English stage. But the former was capable of more fervid brightness in those flashes which characterized the acting of them both. Still, there was something awry within him, which in his body found a visible counterpart. The shapely trunk, crowned with the classic head, was set upon limbs of an ungainly order, short, of coarse vigor, and " gnarled like clumps of oak." Above, all was spiritual; below, of the earth, earthy, and dragging him down. Strong souls, thus inharmoniously embodied, have often developed some irregularity of heart or brain: a disproportion, which only strength of purpose or the most favorable conditions of life could balance and overcome. With the elder Booth, subjected to the varying fortunes and excitements of the early American stage, the evil influence gained sad ascendency, and his finest renditions grew " out of tune and harsh." In depicting the pathetic frenzy of Lear, such actors as he and Kean, when at their best, can surpass all rivals; and the grotesque, darkly powerful ideals of Richard and Shylock are precisely those in which they will startle us to the last, gathering new, though fitful, expressions of hate and scorn, as their own natures sink from ethereal to grosser atmospheres. The mouth catches most surely the growing tendency of a soul; and on

[196]

the lips of the elder Booth there sat a natural half-sneer of pride, which defined the direction in which his genius would reach its farthest scope.

The second picture is a likeness of this great actor's son,—of a face and form now wonted to all who sustain the standard drama of to-day. Here is something of the classic outline and much of the Greek sensuousness of the father's countenance, but each softened and strengthened by the repose of logical thought, and interfused with that serene spirit which lifts the man of feeling so far above the child of passions unrestrained. The forehead is higher, rising toward the region of the moral sentiments; the face is long and oval, such as Ary Scheffer loved to draw; the chin short in height, but, from the ear downwards, lengthening its distinct and graceful curve. The head is of the most refined and thoroughbred Etruscan type, with dark hair thrown backwards and flowing student-wise; the complexion, pale and striking. The eyes are black and luminous, the pupils contrasting sharply with the balls in which they are set. If the profile and forehead evince taste and a balanced mind, it is the hair and complexion, and, above all, those remarkable eyes,—deep-searching, seen and seeing from afar,—that reveal the passions of the father in their heights and depths of power. The form is taller than either that of the elder Booth or Kean, lithe, and disposed in symmetry; with broad shoulders, slender hips, and comely tapering limbs, all supple, and knit together with harmonious grace. We have mentioned personal fitness as a chief badge of the actor's peerage, and it is of one of the born nobility that we have to speak. Amongst those who have few bodily disadvantages to overcome, and who, it would seem, should glide into an assured position more easily than others climb, we may include our foremost American tragedian,— Edwin Thomas Booth.[1]

But men are often endowed with plenteous gifts for which they never find employment, and thus go to the bad without discovering their natural bent to others or even to themselves. In the years preceding our late war how many were rated as vagabonds, who had that within them which has since won renown! They were " born soldiers," and, in the piping time of peace, out of unison with the bustling crowd around them. Life seemed a muddle, and of course they went astray. But when the great guns sounded, and the bugles rang, they came at once to their birthright, and

---

[1] *Not* Edwin *Forrest* Booth, as often and erroneously written. Our actor, born in November, 1833, derived his middle name from Thomas Flyn, the English comedian, his father's contemporary and friend. Edwin was the chosen companion of his father in the latter's tours throughout the United States, and was regarded by the old actor with a strange mixture of repulsion and sympathy,—the one evinced in lack of outward affection and encouragement, the other in a silent but undoubted appreciation of the son's promise. The boy, in turn, so fully understood the father's temperament, that a bond existed between the two. Whether to keep Edwin from the stage, or in caprice, the elder Booth at first rarely permitted the younger to see him act; but the son, attending the father to the theatre, would sit in the wings for hours, listening to the play, and having all its parts so indelibly impressed on his memory as to astonish his brother-actors in later years.

many a ne'er-do-well made himself a patriot and hero forever.

Edwin Booth, having the capabilities of a great actor, found himself about the stage in his childhood, and, by an unwonted kindness of fortune, went through with perhaps the exact training his genius required. If the atmosphere of the theatre had not almost enwrapt his cradle, and thus become a necessity of his after years, his reflective, brooding temperament and æsthetic sensitiveness might have impelled him to one of the silent professions, or kept him an irresolute dreamer through an unsuccessful life. But while his youth was passed in the green-room, a stern discipline early made him self-reliant, matured his powers, taught him executive action, and gave him insight of the passions and manners of our kind. As for black-letter knowledge, such a nature as his was sure to gain that, —to acquire in any event, and almost unknowingly, what mere talent only obtains by severe, methodical application. We know how genius makes unconscious studies, while in the daily routine of life. The soul works on, unassisted, and at length bursts out into sudden blaze. How did Booth study? Just as young Franklin weighed the minister's sermons, while mentally intent upon the architecture of the church roof. Night after night the lonely face brightened the shadows of the stage-wings, and the delicate ear drank in the folly, the feeling, the wit and wisdom of the play. To such a boyhood the personal contact of his father's nature was all in all. It was quaffing from the fountain-head, not from streams of the imitation of imitation. As the genius of the father refined the intellect and judgment of the son, so the weaknesses coupled with that genius taught him strength of character and purpose. We have heard of nothing more dramatic than the wandering companionship of this gifted pair, —whether the younger is awaiting, weary and patient, the end of the heard but unseen play, or watching over his father at a distance, when the clouds settled thickly upon that errant mind, through long nights and along the desolate streets of a strange city. With other years came the time for young Booth to fight his own battle, and wander on his own account through an apprenticeship preceding his mature successes,—to gain those professional acquirements which were needed to complete his education, and to make that tasteful research to which he naturally inclined. He is now in the sunshine of his noonday fame; and we may estimate his measure of excellence by a review of those chosen and successful renderings, that seem most clearly to define his genius, and to mark the limits of height and versatility which he can attain.

Take, then, the part of Hamlet, which, in these days, the very mention of his name suggests. Little remains to be said of that undying play, whose pith and meaning escaped the sturdy English critics, until Coleridge discovered it by looking into his own soul, and those all-searching Germans pierced to the centre of a disposition quite in keeping with their national character. A score of lights have since brought out every thought and phrase, and we now have Hamlet so clearly in our mind's eye as to wonder how our

predecessors failed to comprehend his image. But
what does this tragedy demand of an actor? Pro-
verbially, that he himself shall fill it, and hold the stage
from its commencement to its end. The play of
" Hamlet " is the part of Hamlet. The slowness of
its action, and the import of its dialogue and soliloquies, make all depend upon the central figure. Next,
he is to depict the most accomplished gentleman ever
drawn; not gallant, gay Mercutio, nor courtly Bene-
dict, but the prince and darling of a realm; one who
cannot " lack preferment," being of birth above mean
ambition and self-conscious unrest; a gentleman by
heart, no less,—full of kindly good-fellowship, brook-
ing no titles with his friends, loving goodness and
truth, impatient of fools, scorning affectation; moreover, the glass of fashion and the mould of form, the
modern ideal of manly beauty,—which joins with the
classic face and figure that charm of expression reveal-
ing a delicate mind within. For our Hamlet is both
gentleman and scholar. History and philosophy have
taught him the vice of kings, the brevity of power
and forms, the immortality of principles, the art of
generalization; while contact with society has made
him master of those " shafts of gentle satire," for
which all around him are his unconscious targets.
His self-respect and self-doubt balance each other, until the latter outweighs the former, under the awful
pressure of an unheard-of woe. Finally, he comes
before us in that poetical, speculative period of life
following the years of study and pleasure, and preceding those of executive leadership. Prince, gentle-

man, scholar, poet,—he is each, and all together, and attracts us from every point of view.

Upon this noblest youth—so far in advance of his rude and turbulent time—throw a horror that no philosophy, birth, nor training can resist—one of those weights beneath which all humanity bows shuddering; cast over him a stifling dream, where only the soul can act, and the limbs refuse their offices; have him pushed along by Fate to the lowering, ruinous catastrophe; and you see the dramatic chainwork of a part which he who would enact Hamlet must fulfil.

It has been said, distinguishing between the effects of comedy and tragedy, that to render the latter ennobles actors, so that successful tragedians have acquired graces of personal behavior. ' But one who does not possess native fineness before his portrayal of Hamlet will never be made a gentleman by the part. In its more excited phases, a man not born to the character may succeed. As in Lear, the excess of the passion displayed serves as a mask to the actor's disposition. In its repose, the ideal Hamlet is hard to counterfeit. In the reflective portions and exquisite minor play which largely occupy its progress, and in the princely superiority of its chief figure, there can be little *acting* in the conventional sense. There is a quality which no false ware can imitate. The player must be himself.

This necessity, we think, goes far toward Booth's special fitness for the part. He is in full sympathy with it, whether on or off the stage. We know it from our earliest glance at that lithe and sinuous figure,

elegant in the solemn garb of sables,—at the pallor
of his face and hands, the darkness of his hair, those
eyes that can be so melancholy-sweet, yet ever look
beyond and deeper than the things about him. Where
a burlier tragedian must elaborately pose himself
for the youth he would assume, this actor so easily
and constantly falls into beautiful attitudes and movements, that he seems to go about, as we heard a hu-
morist say, " making statues all over the stage." No
picture can equal the scene where Horatio and Mar-
cellus swear by his sword, he holding the crossed hilt
upright between the two, his head thrown back and
lit with high resolve. In the fencing-bout with Laertes
he is the apotheosis of grace; and since, though his
height and shoulder-breadth are perfect, he is somewhat spare in form, you call to mind—in accounting
for this charm of motion, not studied, " like old Hay-
ward's, between two looking-glasses "—the law that
beauty is frame-deep; that grace results from the conscious, harmonious adjustment of joints and bones,
and not from accidental increase and decrease of their
covering. There is more hidden art in his sitting attitudes upon the quaint lounges of the period; whether
rebuking his own remissness, or listening to " the
rugged Pyrrhus," or playing upon old Polonius,—setting his breast, as it were, against the thorn of his
own disgust.

A sense of the fitness of things makes Booth hold
himself in close restraint when not engaged upon the
sharper crises of the play. This we conceive to be
the true art-spirit. There is no attempt to rouse the

house by elocutionary climaxes or quick-stopping strides. Like Betterton, he courts rapturous silence rather than clamorous applause. So finished is all this as a study, that the changes into the more dramatic passages at first grate harshly upon the eye and ear. For, after all, it is a tragedy, full of spectral terrors. Lord Hamlet feels it in his soul. Why should this delicate life be so rudely freighted? Booth, faithful to the action, accepts the passion and the pang. We hardly relish his gasping utterance and utter fall, when the Ghost rehearses his story on those solemn battlements of Elsinore. But think what he is seeing: not the stage-vision for which we care so little, but the spectre of his father,—a midnight visitant from the grave! It has been asserted that no man ever *believed* he saw a spirit and survived the shock. And it is strongly urged, as a defence of Booth's conception of this scene, that, in the closet interview with the Queen, after the slaying of Polonius, and on the Ghost's reappearance, we, now wrought up to the high poetic pitch by the dialogue and catastrophe, and by the whole progress of the piece, ourselves catch the key, expect, and fully sympathize with his horror and prostration, and accept the fall to earth as the proper sequel to that dreadful blazon from the other world. Notwithstanding this, it seems to us that Booth should tone down his manner in the first Act. The audience has hardly left the outer life, and cannot identify itself with the player; and an artist must acknowledge this fact, and not too far exceed the elevation of his hearers.

Five years ago there was a weakness in Booth's

voice, making the listener apprehensive of the higher and louder tones. This insufficiency has passed away with practice and growth, and his utterance now has precisely the volume required in Hamlet,—being musical and distinct in the quiet parts, and fully sustaining each emotional outburst.

In effective compositions there is a return to the theme or refrain of the piece, when the end is close upon us. One of the finest points in this play is, that after the successive episodes of the killing of Polonius, the madness and death of Ophelia, and the wild bout with Laertes at her burial, Hamlet reassumes his everyday nature, and is never more thoroughly himself than when Osric summons him to the fencing-match, and his heart grows ill with the shadow of coming death. The Fates are just severing his thread; events that shall sweep a whole dynasty, like the house of Atreus, into one common ruin, are close at hand; but Philosophy hovers around her gallant child, and the sweet, wise voice utters her teachings for the last time: "If it be now, 'tis not to come; if it be not to come, it will be now; if it be not now, yet it will come; the readiness is all. Let be." Then follow the courtesy, the grace, the fraud, the justice, of the swift, last scene; the curtain falls; and now the yearning sympathies of the hearers break out into sound, and the actor comes before the footlights to receive his meed of praise. How commonplace it is to read that such a one was called before the curtain and bowed his thanks! But sit there; listen to the applauding clamor of two thousand voices, be yourself lifted on the waves of that exultation, and for a moment you forget how soon all this will be hushed forever, and, in the triumph of the actor, the grander, more enduring genius of the writer whose imagination first evoked the spell.

The performance of Richelieu, from one point of view, is a complete antithesis to that of the melancholy Dane. In the latter we see and think of Booth; in the former, his household friends, watching My Lord Cardinal from first to last, have nothing to recall him to their minds. The man is transformed, is *acting* throughout the play. Voice, form and countenance are changed; only the eyes remain, and they are volcanic with strange lustre,—mindful of the past, suspicious of the present, fixed still upon the future with piercing intent. The soul of the Cardinal, nearing its leave of the tenement that has served it so long, glares out of the windows, with supernatural regard, over the luxury, the intrigue, the danger, the politics, the empire it must soon behold no more. As the piece is now produced, with fidelity to details of use and decoration,— with armor, costumery, furniture and music of the period of Louis XIII.,—with all this boast of heraldry and pomp of power, the illusion is most entire. The countenance is that of the old portrait; white flowing locks, cap, robes, raised mustache, and pointed beard, —all are there. The voice is an old man's husky treble, and we have the old man's step, the tremor, and recurring spasmodic power; nor is there any moment when the actor forgets the part he has assumed. Yes, it is age itself; but the sunset of a life whose noonday was gallantry, valor, strength,—and intellectual strength never so much as now. How we lend our own impulses to the effort with which the veteran grasps the sword wherewith he shore " the stalwart Englisher," strive with him in that strong yearning to whirl it aloft, sink with him in the instant, nerveless reaction, and sorrow that "a child could slay Richelieu now!" He is not the intriguer of dark tradition, wily and cruel for low ambitious ends, but entirely great, in his protection of innocence and longing for affection, and most of all in that supreme love of France to which his other motives are subservient. Booth seizes upon this as the key-note of the play, and is never so grand as when he rises at full height with the averment,

> I found France rent asunder;
> The rich men despots, and the poor banditti;
> Sloth in the mart, and schism within the temple;
> Brawls festering to rebellion, and weak laws
> Rotting away with rust in antique sheaths,—
> *I have re-created France!*

Bulwer's *Richelieu,* though written in that author's pedantic, artificial manner, and catching the groundlings with cheap sentiment and rhetorical platitudes, is yet full of telling dramatic effects, which, through the inspiration of a fine actor, lift the most critical audience to sudden heights. One of this sort is justly famous. We moderns, who so feebly catch the spell which made the Church of Rome sovereign of sovereigns for a thousand years, have it cast full upon us in the scene where the Cardinal, deprived of temporal power, and defending his beautiful ward from royalty itself, draws around her that Church's "awful circle," and cries to Baradas,

> Set but a foot within that holy ground,
> And on thy head—yea, though it wore a crown—
> *I launch the curse of Rome!*

Booth's expression of this climax is wonderful. There is perhaps nothing, of its own kind, to equal it upon the present stage. Well may the king's haughty parasites cower, and shrink aghast from the ominous voice, the finger of doom, the arrows of those lurid, unbearable eyes! But it is in certain intellectual elements and pathetic undertones that the part of Richelieu, as conceived by Bulwer, assimilates to that of Hamlet, and comes within the realm where our actor's genius holds assured sway. The argument of the piece is spiritual power. The body of Richelieu is wasted, but the soul remains unscathed, with all its reason, passion, and indomitable will. He is still prelate, statesman and poet, and equal to a world in arms.

The requisite subtilty of analysis, and sympathy with mental finesse, must also specially adapt this actor to the correct assumption of the character of Iago. Those who have never seen him in it may know by analogy that his merits are not exaggerated. We take it that Iago is a sharply intellectual personage, though his logic, warped by grovelling purpose, becomes sophistry, while lustful and envious intrigues occupy his skilful brain. We have described the beauty of Booth's countenance in repose. But it is equally remarkable for mobility, and his most expressive results are produced by liftings of the high-arched brows and the play of passions about the flexible mouth. The natural line of his lip, not scornful in itself, is on that straight border-ground where a hair's breadth can raise it into sardonic curves, transforming all its good to sneering evil. In his rendering, Iago must become a shining, central incarnation of tempting deceit, with Othello's generous nature a mere puppet in his hands. As Richard III., we should look to find him most effective in schemeful soliloquy and the phases of assumed virtue and affection, while perhaps less eminent than his father or Edmund Kean in that headlong, strident unrest, which hurried on their representations to the fury of the retributive end.

To give the distant reader our own impression of a great actor is a slow and delicate task, and perhaps the most we can accomplish is to set him before others somewhat as he has appeared to us, and to let each decide for himself the question of histrionic rank. But have we not unconsciously defined our view of the excellence of Booth's genius, and hinted at its limitations? The latter are by no means narrow, for his elastic, adaptable nature insures him versatility; and, despite the world's scepticism as to the gift of an artist to do more than one thing well, he is acknowledged to surpass our other actors in a score of elegant parts. Amongst these are Pescara, Petruchio, and Sir Edward Mortimer; while in a few pieces of the French romance-school, such as *Ruy Blas,* and that terrible *The King's Jester,* he has introduced to us studies

[209]

of a novel and intensely dramatic kind. As for the lighter order, the greater including the less, our best Hamlet should be the best " walking gentleman," if he elect to assume that versatile personage's offices. We know also that Booth's Shylock should be a masterly performance, since his voice, complexion, eyes, and inherited powers of scorn, all lend their aid to his mental appreciation of the part. But it is not our purpose to consider any of these *rôles*. We only allude to them to say that in most directions his equal has not appeared on the American stage; and in qualifying an opinion of his powers, we make no exception in favor of his contemporaries, but, rather, of those who have been and shall be again, when Jove shall

> let down from his golden chain
> An age of better metal.

As Hamlet, Mr. Booth will hardly improve his present execution, since he is now at the age of thirty-two, and can never fill more easily the youthful beauty of the part, without artifice, and, we may say, by the first intention. We should like to see him, ere many winters have passed over his head, in some new classic play, whose arrangement should not be confined to the bald, antique model, nor drawn out in sounding speeches like Talfourd's " Ion," nor yet too much infused with the mingled Gothic elements of our own drama; but warm with sunlight, magical with the grace of the young Athenian feeling, and full of a healthful action which would display the fairest endowments of his mind and person. As Lear or Shylock, he will certainly grow in power as he grows in years, and may even gain upon his masterly performance of Richelieu. But in one department, and that of an important order, he will perhaps never reach the special eminence at which we place a few historic names.

Our exception includes those simply powerful characters, the ideal of which his voice and magnetism cannot in themselves sustain. At certain lofty passages he relies upon nervous, electrical effort, the natural weight of his temperament being unequal to the desired end. Those flashing impulses, so compatible with the years of Richelieu and the galled purpose of Shylock, would fail to reveal satisfactorily the massive types, which rise by a head, like Agamemnon, above the noblest host. Dramatic representations may be classed under the analogous divisions of poetry: for instance, the satirical, the bucolic, the romantic, the reflective, the epic. The latter has to do with those towering creatures of action—Othello, Coriolanus, Virginius, Macbeth—somewhat deficient, whether good or evil, in the casuistry of more subtile dispositions, but giants in emotion, and kingly in repose. They are essentially *masculine,* and we connect their ideals with the stately figure, the deep chest-utterance, the slow, enduring majesty of mien. The genius of Mr. Booth has that feminine quality which, though allowing him a wider range, and enabling him to render even these excepted parts after a tuneful, elaborate, and never ignoble method of his own, might debar him from giving them their highest interpretation,—or, at least, from sustaining it, without sharp

[211]

falsetto effort, throughout the entire passage of a play. In a few impersonations, where Kemble, with all his mannerisms and defective elocution, and Macready, notwithstanding his uninspired, didactic nature, were most at their ease and successful, this actor would be somewhat put to his mettle,—a fact of which he is probably himself no less aware.

After all, what are we saying, except that his genius is rather Corinthian than Doric, and therefore more cultured, mobile, and of wider range? If Kemble was the ideal Coriolanus and Henry V., he was too kingly as Hamlet, and Booth is the *princeliest* Hamlet that ever trod the stage. If Kean and the elder Booth were more supernal in their lightnings of passion and scorn,—and there are points in *Richelieu* which leave this a debatable question,—Edwin Booth is more equal throughout, has every resource of taste and study at his command; his action is finished to the last, his stage-business perfect, his reading distinct and musical as a bell. He is thus the ripened product of our eclectic later age, and has this advantage about him, being an American, that he is many-sided, and draws from all foreign schools their distinctive elements to fuse into one new, harmonious whole.

It is our fashion to speak of the decline of the Drama, to lament not only a decay of morals, manners, and elocution, but the desertion of standard excellence for the frippery which only appeals to the lightest popular taste. But this outcry proceeds mostly from old fogies, and those who only reverence the past, while the halo which gilds the memories of youth is the cause of its ceaseless repetition. For it has been heard through every period. It was in the era when our greatest dramas were created that Ben Jonson, during a fit of the spleen, occasioned by the failure of *The New Inn,* begat these verses " to himself ":—

> Come, leave the loathed stage,
> And this more loathsome age,
> Where pride and impudence, in faction knit,
> Usurp the chair of wit!
> Inditing and arranging every day
> Something they call a play.

At the commencement of our own century, and in what we are wont to consider the Roscian Period of the British stage, its condition seemed so deplorable to Leigh Hunt, then the dramatic critic of *The News,* as to require " An Essay on the Appearance, Causes, and Consequences of the Decline of British Comedy." " Of Tragedy," he wrote, " we have nothing; and it is the observation of all Europe that the British Drama is rapidly declining." Yet the golden reign of the Kembles was then in its prime; and such names as Bannister, Fawcett, Matthews, Elliston, and Cooke occur in Hunt's graceful and authoritative sketches of the actors of the day.[1] As to the newer plays, Gifford said, " All the fools in the kingdom seem to have exclaimed with one voice, Let us write for the theatre! " Latter-day croakers would have us believe that the

[1] *Critical Essays on the Performers of the London Theatres, Including General Observations on the Practice and Genius of the Stage.* London, 1807. Some publisher would do well to give us a reprint of this noted collection.

Tragic Muse, indignant at the desecration of her English altars, took flight across the ocean, alighting in solemn majesty at the Old Park Theatre of New York, but that she disappeared utterly in the final conflagration of that histrionic shrine. Well, there are smouldering remnants of the Old Park still left to us; veteran retainers of the conventional stride, the disdainful gesture, the Kemble elocution, and that accent which was justly characterized as

Ojus, insijjus, hijjus, and perfijjus!

But the Muse is immortal, though so changing the fashion of her garb, it would appear, as often to fail of recognition from ancient friends. We think that modern acting is quite as true to nature as that of the school which has passed away, while its accessories are infinitely richer and more appropriate; and as to the popular judgment, how should that be on the decline? In America,—where common wealth makes common entrance, and the lines are not so clearly drawn between the unskilful many and the judicious few,—managers will always make concessions to the whim and folly of the hour. But we see no cause for discouragement, so long as dramas are set forth with the conscientious accuracy that has marked the latest productions of *Hamlet* and *Richelieu*, and while hushed and delighted audiences, drawn from every condition of society, leave all meaner performances to hang upon the looks and accents of Nature's sweet interpreter,—Edwin Booth.

XVII

KING—"THE FROLIC AND THE GENTLE"[1]

FROM the first he had the grace to put me on close terms with him, although we seldom met when he had not just come from a distant region or was departing for some other point as far. In this wise, I could not free myself from the illusion that he was a kind of Martian—a planetary visitor, of a texture differing from that of ordinary Earth-dwellers. It seemed quite natural that he should map out the globe, and bore through it to see of what it was made. Now that he is gone, I am still looking for his casual return.

There was one occasion which I did not share with others of his present celebrants; a period when I had him to myself, and when he began an episode eventful in even his own full life. This was nothing less than that of his initial visit to the Old World. By chance, with a son in his first year out from Yale, I left New York, in the spring of 1882, on the same steamer which numbered on its passenger-roll Clarence King, and another mining-expert, at that time his partner. Of course I had read with admiration, a decade earlier, the *Mountaineering in the Sierra Nevada,* and often had wondered why its luminous author had not shone continuously in our literature. I should have

[1] From *Clarence King Memoirs.* The King Memorial Committee of the Century Association, 1904.

[215]

wondered the more that I had never met him, had I
not seen his name figuring in those society lists that
were quite alien to my quiet round of life. But at
dinner we were at the same table. He was good
enough to make the advance, and to claim a whimsical
consanguinity on the score of our Clarentian prenom-
ina. Now, I knew that he was a famous government
geodeticist, but had no conception of his temperament. Perhaps he took me with equal seriousness.
At all events, he was more on his dignity, or gravity,
than I ever afterward saw him. In the starry evening
we walked the deck together, and talked of public
affairs, books, etc., soon wandering to scientific research and discovery, concerning which I eagerly lis-
tened to his theories of matter, vortex rings, the
Earth's structure, the chances of a future life. I doubt
if there was a laugh between us, and am sure that I
never again found him so long in one humor. Nor
was there anything in this thorough-bred, travel-
dressed, cosmopolitan to suggest that he had not spent
repeated seasons upon the hemisphere to which we
were bound.

Out on the blue, the next morning, what a trans-
formation! As I have said, it was in fact King's
first opportunity to visit Europe, strictly off duty, and
with means that seemed to him beyond the dreams of
avarice. He broke out into a thousand pranks and
paradoxes. Freedom was what we both needed, and
my own reserve was at an end the moment I saw him
changed from the dignitary to a veritable Prince
Florizel with the tray of tarts, offering lollipops right

and left. He and his comrade, I was speedily made to know, had "struck it rich" in a mine and were independent for life. His motto for one summer at least was "*Vive la bagatelle.*" His frolic was incessant and contagious. Here was my overnight philosopher with double-eagles in his pocket, one of which he periodically flipped in the air to decide wagers made upon every possible pretext between himself and his decidedly less buoyant colleague. He jested, fabled, sparkled, scorned concealment of his delight. Indeed, I verily believe that I then had the rare fortune, at the beginning of our friendship, first, to learn the resources and conviction of his noble mind, and in a trice to enjoy the ebullition of his mirth and fancy on some of the happiest days of his existence.

He had with him a Gargantuan letter of credit. From a slip in his wallet he took and showed me a single draft for a thousand pounds, a very sacred special fund, which was to be piously expended for some one work of art, his roc's egg, his supreme trophy— in fine, the most beauteous and essential thing he might come upon in this tour. All this as gravely as if he were a Knight of the Grail, or meditating in the end to shift to America the Hotel Cluny or a court of the Alhambra.

Among the many wagers which he forced his staid comrade to accept was one that compelled the loser to take the four of us, young and old, to Epsom on the Derby Day that would occur soon after our arrival in London. King lost this bet, plainly by his own intent. Everything was to come off in the traditional style—that the Scriptures might be fulfilled to the uttermost, as indeed they were. From the White Horse Inn, Piccadilly, a fortnight later, we took the road and shared its carnival, on the finest tallyho obtainable; whip, guard, lackey, hampers and all. Nothing was omitted in the going and coming. It was a brilliant day; our coach rounded to in the center of the field, as in Frith's picture, and there were the gipsy tumblers on the green, the lunchers, the Prince of Wales, the race—with the Duke of Westminster's colors to the fore. Yes, and we saw a welcher mobbed, and everything else was accomplished; and I still cherish a fading tin-type exhibit of our group on the tallyho, lifting our cups, with King as toastmaster.

Our Prince of paradox would not bide another day in London, but sped to France, leaving me a bearer of ill tidings to those who knew he was coming, and whose desire to welcome him taught me that he was an international character. When I overtook him in Paris he was on the eve of going to his longed-for Spain; not, indeed, to tarry even there, but to push right through to Morocco or Algeria, upon the trail of a certain unique shawl, or curtain, or tapestry, which he alone must possess. Of his return to Spain, his social life in France, his conquest of England, his blood-brotherhood with Ferdinand Rothschild, and of the *spolia opima* brought back to America,—are they not all written in the book of the hearts that held him dear?

Thus have I told how Pantagruel found Panurge, whom he loved all his life thereafter. I do not know whether it was on this ornamental journey that Clarence King's genius led him to the imperishable Helmet of Mambrino, now hung (by proxy) from its arm of wrought iron in the upper chambers of the Century. Whether it was then or afterward that he conceived his epistle to Don Horacio, and therewith imprisoned the very soul of Spain in the flask of his translucent English, the feat was equally enduring. Nothing comparable to the flavor of his style is to be found elsewhere, unless in the fantasy of his fellow-Centurion to whose loiterings in Mexico we owe " San Antonio of the Gardens" and successive companion-pieces. King's speech and writ were iridescent with the imagination of the born romancer. Judge of the statue by the fragment, and think of what was lost to literature by the fact that it was not his vocation, but his accomplishment. Nor was it his lot to escape enrollment with the inheritors of unfulfilled renown by winning, like the most distinguished of his poet friends, a place in history as one of the arbiters of civilization, and one of those who shape the destinies of their own lands. None the less, the by-play of some men has a quality unattained by a host of devotees who make its acquisition the labor of their workaday lives.

Quis desiderio sit pudor! As I humbly stood on one side, that arctic morning when the choice and true followed his remains down the aisle, I knew that deep in the souls of all, however freezing the bitter wind, the memory of King was enshrined forever, and that his Manes would have no cause to make complaint of benefits forgot.

[219]

XVIII

GUY WETMORE CARRYL [1]

IF Guy Carryl had belonged to an earlier generation, it may be conjectured that he would have become known chiefly as a poet. Such more certainly would have been the case if he had grown up in rural life, apart from the opportunities for general literary work that, as it were, came to him from the first. The lyrical bent was strong within him. This might almost be inferred from one little poem which he wrote, while still a lad, on the death of a child. It contains a tender conceit, expressed with the grace and feeling that have warranted its preservation in a collection of his maturer serious verse.

His early writings, grave or gay, were often in metrical form, but none of the self-conscious type that marks the callow dreamer. They were the bright improvisations of a young man who inherited, besides the poet's ear and voice, a sense of the mirthful, and the impulse to fashion whatever could lighten the heart of a child, or "that child's heart within the man's" which even the luckless still retain. The bulk of his diversified and abundant early work was of

[1] Preface to *The Garden of Years, and Other Poems.* New York: G. P. Putnam's Sons, 1904.

the most buoyant nature possible. It could scarcely have been otherwise, with his unique facility and irrepressible zest in life.

Life must have seemed very fair to him, as he himself seemed to others, when I first knew him in his student days. He did everything with a happy ease, and was apparently without a care. Handsome, healthy, debonair,—a youth in years and bearing, a man in his accomplishments,—he surely was Fortune's favorite. I remember his many graces, and the sparkling quality of the plays that he wrote, and that proved so apt when enacted by fellow-students or by the associations for which some of them were cast. With all his relish for life, he was steadfastly ambitious, and the reverse of an idler devoted to pleasures everywhere within his reach. Still, in the strength of his youth, he seemed quite equal to either experience or work, and likely to take his fill of both.

This he succeeded in doing, as a poet, an observer, a journalist, a novelist, a man in touch with his comrades and the world. The present collection embraces the poems which he had begun to arrange, substantially as here given, and which may be considered expressive of his most elevated moods. They were the overflow of a talent that was largely occupied with lighter work, or, most of all, in the prose fiction by which he gained, and was increasing, his hold upon public favor. In the thought of all that might have been the outcome of after years, I am moved by the pity of their denial. As it is, the hands of his elders set the lamp on the stone that bears his name,—a service which, had not the order of things been thus reversed, he would not have failed, in their behalf, to render.

A young author traditionally catches some manner of his time that most appeals to him. Such has been the wont of poets who have lived to institute, in their turn, new modes, and to have their own followers. During the brief tenure of Guy Carryl's activity two opposing tendencies of verse have been much in vogue. One of these betrays a lack of feeling and spontaneity through its curious elaboration, and has been frankly termed, by its votaries, the decadent song of a dying century. At the other extreme is the virile, perhaps too careless, balladry of which the English imperialist poet is the forceful exemplar. It may be placed to the credit of the author of this volume that,—despite his attachment for France and her literature, and his residence in Paris during impressible years,—his verse is in nowise decadent; it betrays hardly a trace of the symbolist diction so little in accord with the genius of our English tongue. His ballads—and he is at his best in these—have the ring of a manful and genuinely American songster. They are what such a one might well compose at the outset of a new century, and in a country of the future. Nearly all of this verse is in the major key. Even its brooding sentiment is that of a live man and no weakling.

Byron was a live man, and, to the end, a young man, never more so than when he thought himself otherwise. If it were just to apply a single epithet to the titular poem of this volume, it might be termed

Byronic; for it is full of the Haroldian spirit of youth,
—never more so than when its writer, at that stage
where a man feels older than he ever again will feel
until reaching his grand climacteric, breaks forth with
" Heart of my heart, I am no longer young!" He
revels, besides, like the Georgian pilgrim, in the sense
of freedom, as he goes oversea to test the further
world. "The Garden of Years" is a love poem; but
its emotion is a warm under-color, toning a novice's
pictures of travel during his wander-year. Tech-
nically, the poem is cast in an original stanzaic form,
effectively maintained from beginning to end.

This prelude is not a criticism, but a tribute of affection and remembrance. Readers who care for poetry will at once observe that a certain lyrical eloquence
is a general characteristic of " The Garden of Years "
and the ensuing shorter pieces, charged with a passion
for Nature and a spirit of intense sympathy with their
author's fellow-men. Equally manifest is his versatility, shown by the exultant tone of the hymn of re-
habilitation, " Gloria Mundi," the tenderness of " At
Twilight," and the light touch of " The Débutante,"
—a range even more striking when contrasted with
the whimsical drollery of his published volumes of
humorous verse. He did right in grouping together
the five ballads that follow the title-poem; and in so
doing emphasized not only their strength, but the
patriotism which was one of his most attractive traits.
Proud of his country's victories, American to the core,
he is nowhere more impulsive than in the fine lyric,
" When the Great Gray Ships Come in," which sings

of peace rather than of war. It expresses, no less, his
passion for the sea and his comprehension of it. Like
that older bard of our Eastern Coast, he had the key to
ocean's book of mystery; he loved its tides and eddies,
the shells and flotsam along its shores, its laughter and
mist and surge. The ships upon its bosom, the dere-
licts that never reached their "Haven-Mother,"
charmed his imagination. Finally, one may note how,
throughout his swift and crowded experience, his sense
of reverence was never dulled. The lines entitled
"The Winds and the Sea Obey Him" came from no
frivolous heart. As he looked out upon the waters, he
was moved to write that "amid a vexing multitude
of creeds" his faith abided still. "The Spirit of Mid-
Ocean"—at once his valediction and a vivid token
of his birthright as a poet—closes with unaffected
homage to the Source whence inspiration flows to every
soul—to each according to his degree and need:

Hush! If this be the servant, what must the Master be?

XIX

TREASURE TOMBS AT MYKENÆ [1]

IN the following article I endeavor to give a statement of the significance, from a literary point of
view, of the remarkable discoveries thus far made by
Dr. Schliemann in his explorations at the site of Mykenæ. In order to do this we must recur to the epics
of Homer and the majestic drama of the Attic
tragedians—to the poetry of a race which has fur-
nished the most exquisite models of all succeeding
verse.

Children, reading translations of Homer with delight, yield by instinct to the charm of his matchless
beauty and simplicity. They no more question his narrative than they doubt the histories of Cæsar and Napoleon, the voyages of Dampier, or the tales of the
Conquistadores. But the most of us, when once past
the age of faith in fairy-land and fable, have classed
the songs of the wrath and valor of Achilles, the wit
and wanderings of Odysseus, and the woes of the house
of Atreus, among the more doubtful legends belong-
ing to the youth of the world. The theories of Heyne,
Wolf, and their pupils, which made the Homeric
poems a growth or collection, rather than a personal
composition, have caused us almost to distrust the in-

[1] *New York Daily Tribune,* January 13, 1877.

dividuality of Homer himself. The best scholars have become reluctant to give any credence to the historical import of the Iliad and Odyssey, and indeed of the glorious procession of the Athenian masterpieces, whose themes were largely taken from the episodes and traditions gathered in the measures of the blind Ionian bard. The geography and narrative of Herodotos were long under a similar cloud. The known absurdities gravely interspersed throughout his history stamped him as a marvel-monger, and served to vitiate the entire record of the Pierian books.

But in our own time a change has marked the opinion of the critical world. The exact research of modern travellers and geographers has proved that Herodotos, while overcredulous in minor and hearsay matters, was correct in essentials, even to the general topography and ethnology of the remote portions of Central Africa. And as for Homer, we begin to see in his poems a single creation, rather than a growth, and again to conceive of his simple and poetic individuality,—a blind, gray-bearded, heaven-endowed minstrel, wandering from Smyrna to Greece, and there from province to province, idealizing the history of his heroic period and race, and, either by oral or scriptural methods, fastening his ballad-epics upon time itself, so that, handed down from sire to son, they became the enduring treasure of all generations of mankind. We begin to feel—making allowance for the supernaturalism of an age when nothing was known of the earth itself, beyond the pillars of Herakles on the West and the Ganges on the East—when the gods were thought to be the progenitors and companions of men —allowing for this we not only begin to feel that the Iliad and Odyssey are true to the physical status of the Mediterranean islands and shores, but we more than suspect that their stories of wars and warriors, of voyages, sieges, and of civil and domestic life, are the narratives of actual matters which were of the highest relative importance in a half-barbaric age; lastly, we look backward to find that Homer's personages were living, loving, warring, human beings, and that, while yet scarcely having left the flesh, their deeds and sayings, by turns wise and paltry, joyous and tragical, were the most exciting themes of the minstrel of that ancient time.

One of *The Tribune's* writers has well said that it is indeed a most fortunate thing that this man of our time *has believed in Homer;* that Dr. Schliemann was so impressed in youth with faith in the reality of the actions and manners depicted in the Ionic verse as to acquire a fortune with purpose to become an explorer, and to prove by his own exertions the general historic truth of the Iliad and Odyssey. There has been much dispute over his achievements in the Troad. The spot selected, after preliminary experiments elsewhere, for his serious efforts to uncover the ruins of Troia, was chosen against the judgment of many scholars. The unearthed relics, although marked with the sun-emblem which might typify the name of Ilios, were not of such a character as at once to remove all scepticism from European archæologists. Even in his own country his reports were received with criticism. Worn down by fever contracted on the banks of the Simois and Scamander, and hindered by the distrust of the Turkish authorities, he transferred the scene of his operations to Greece. Here Curtius has been achieving wonders at Olympia, and restoring to light the buried temples and effigies of all Olympos' hierarchy. But the disciple of Homer has undertaken labors that make the field of Olympian researches seem comparatively modern, and now startles the reading world with the progress of his work at Mykenæ—a city destroyed by the Argives in the century after the erection of Olympia's first temple—a city whose king was the most powerful chieftain in Greece at the time when, with the collected Grecian fleet and more than a hundred thousand warriors, he sailed from Aulis to recover Helena and demolish the " lofty walls of Troy."

Among our own experts, Bayard Taylor, the traveller, poet, and Hellenist, was one who fully and heartily declared his belief that Dr. Schliemann had discovered the true site of Ilion. His essay, which first appeared in *The Tribune*, was the most complete and pronounced of all the tributes awarded to the discoverer, and greatly encouraged him to continue in his chosen career.

No coldness, in America at least, attended the reception of the news from Mykenæ which reached us on the 10th of December. *The Herald* of that Sunday contained a telegraphic report of Schliemann's dispatch to the King of Greece, dated November 28, and I think that the heart of each lover of learning, art, or song, leapt with wonder and something like delight, accepting the genuineness and importance of the results obtained and the promise given out. It was felt that here was something substantial. There is no dispute over the *site* of Mykenæ, as over that of Troy. The Cyclopean ruins, described by Pausanias 17 centuries ago, are still partly visible to the traveller. The oral and written tradition of his time assumed them to be the very walls and monuments of Agamemnon's city, and, if they were not, their *vraisemblance* was the image of reality itself. According to the chronology which scholars usually adopt, Mykenæ was at its prime B.C. 1184—the date of the fall of Troy. It was destroyed by the Argives B.C. 468, 2,344 years ago, and there is no historic evidence that a new city was built upon its ruins. All this rendered it the more probable that under the dust of centuries Schliemann might have found, in comparative preservation, the vaults and secret treasure-houses of the early chiefs of Argolis—possibly the once revered tomb of the King of Men himself. In a later dispatch we learn that Schliemann thinks the site was again peopled, and that an Argive city existed there for a long time, because the surface of the ground is full of the remains of a Greek age. On the 19th of November he had discovered enormous tombs, at the depth of 25 feet, surrounded by parallel Cyclopean walls; on the 24th he opened two more, which contained the bones of a man and a woman, and from these and adjoining vaults he obtained a vast amount of archælogical treasure—urns, vases, sculp-

tures, diadems, masks, domestic implements, sceptres
—much of it pure gold, the rest composed of bronze,
silver, and even of crystal and precious stones. The
details of this marvellous " find " were but briefly indicated in his hurried letter to King George, in which
he waived all claim to the treasure, " sufficient to fill
a large museum, and the most splendid in the world,"
and offered it " with intense enthusiasm, entirely to
Greece."

Later dispatches enumerate the articles found and
fully confirm the assertion of the explorer, besides
giving a more elaborate description of the position
and character of the tombs thus opened. But when
the first news crossed the Atlantic, it was felt, I say,
that here was something of priceless meaning, and our
own people were moved to something of the " enthusiasm " displayed by the joyous discoverer himself. True, he had used similar language in respect
to what seemed to us the less assured triumph of his
labors in the Troad. But it is this unbounded eagerness and delight which go to the making of a great
explorer and finally produce splendid results. There
is always a sufficient number of critics icily cold to
freeze out those who are pretenders; and when a
worthy aspirant appears, it requires all the energy of a
strong nature to sustain before them his heat and noble
rage.

The interest taken by our intelligent public in the
news from Mykenæ at once found expression in the
daily journals. Let me allude to the amusing and
somewhat provincial inconsistency of our English

cousins in their comments upon our acquaintance with those paths of culture to which they have long been wonted, and which are supposed to lead to sweetness and light. For years they have accused us of too much pedantry and refinement in our life and letters. They have deprecated our hankering for the methods and relics of the Old World, for " the glory that was Greece and the grandeur that was Rome." They have berated us for neglecting the home field, for our inability to discover American themes and properly treat them. Yet when some veritable success is reached by Americans in a field of which they claim the usufruct, they strike a different attitude, and we are treated to sneers at our ignorance, boorishness, and lack of scholastic feeling. It may be, as *The Saturday Review* implies, that it was necessary for us to purchase the Cesnola collection, seeing that therefrom, " as years roll on, American ladies will learn that Phœnician is not the European way of pronouncing Venetian, and popular education will thrive immensely." But the majority of the readers of *The Tribune* are more familiar with the geography of Europe than any thousand men you can find in London are with that of these United States. I need not speak of the additional charm which for us our very isolation bestows upon the antique. But let me cite a fact which has its application. I am told that in this modern mercantile city of New York a " Greek Club " has been in healthful and vigorous existence for the last nineteen years. It consists of a dozen gentlemen, gathered from various callings, who meet weekly at one another's houses, during the winter months, and read the texts not only of the purest and most famous authors but of the minor relics of the Greek tongue. Doubtless some of these gentlemen, if we seek no further, will be able to enjoy and study intelligently the coming Cyprian antiquities, and doubtless there are others of their breed, even in our frontier towns, who take a lively interest in the researches of Curtius and Schliemann. It was a citizen of New Hampshire who assisted Di Cesnola, at the most trying period of his undertaking, with friendship, presence, and material aid. If any country has a better right than our own to the purchase of treasures unearthed by an American consul, who depended largely on America for his resources, let its learned representatives now speak or else hereafter forever hold their peace.

We come to the dramatic suggestiveness of Schliemann's discoveries, in their bearing upon the history and literature of ancient Greece. Agamemnon, the King of Men, son of Atreus, brother of Menelaös of Sparta, lord of Mykenæ, and called by Homer the " ruler of many islands and of all Argos," is the heroic central figure—or figurehead—of the Homeric poems, as the leader of all Greece against Troy. In the Iliad he acts as a presiding genius, towering above the host as Saul above the people, the emblem of sovereignty and justice. The entire epos of that poem grows out of the dispute between him and Achilles as to the possession of Briseis. After the fall of Troy, the prophetess Kassandra, daughter of Priam, became the captive mistress of Agamemnon, and, according to tradition, warned him against returning to Mykenæ. In the Odyssey, the story of his death is told and retold at different stages of the poem. Ægisthos had been left in " horse-pasturing Argos," by the king, as his viceroy, during the war. As years rolled on the treacherous cousin succeeded in gaining the guilty love of Klytæmnestra, wife to Agamemnon, and the pair seized upon the kingdom as their own. Fearing the wrath of the injured chieftain, they conspired to murder him upon his return. Of this tragedy we have two accounts—the epic and the dramatic. According to Homer, Ægisthos, when notified of Agamemnon's arrival with but a handful of his troop, went forth to welcome him, and to invite him to his mansion. There he fell upon him at a banquet, and slaughtered him and all his companions, including the royal captive, Kassandra. The fullest Odyssean version is to be found in the Eleventh Book, wherein Odysseus relates to Alkinoös the story of his wanderings subsequent to the war. He recounts his visit to the ghostly land of the Kimmerii, and the incantations which brought to him the souls of the dead.

This passage I translate from the text of Dindorf (somewhat hastily, but with due regard to literalness), into that English measure of six feet, which, although very different from the classical and quantitative hexameter, is thought by Matthew Arnold to be the one which most nearly imitates the unceasing rapid current of the Homeric song, and in which we can best preserve the stress of minor words and particles, and

render by an equal number of English lines the verse
of the original:

THE DEATH OF AGAMEMNON

[*Odyssey, XI.,* 385-456.]

Afterward, soon as the chaste Persephone hither and
  thither
Now had scattered afar the slender shades of the women,
Came the sorrowing ghost of Agamemnon Atreides;
Round whom thronged, besides, the souls of the others
  who also
Died, and met their fate, with him in the house of Ægis-
  thos.
He, then, after he drank of the dark blood, instantly
  knew me,—
Ay, and he wailed aloud, and plenteous tears was shed-
  ding,
Toward me reaching hands and eagerly longing to touch
  me;
But he was shorn of strength, nor longer came at his bid-
  ding
That great force which once abode in his pliant men-
  bers.
Seeing him thus, I wept, and my heart was laden with
  pity,
And, uplifting my voice, in wingéd words I addressed
  him:
  " King of men, Agamemnon, thou glorious son of
  Atreus,
Say, in what wise did the doom of prostrate death over-
  come thee?
Was it within thy ships thou wast subdued by Poseidon
Rousing the dreadful blast of winds too hard to be mas-
  tered,
Or on the firm-set land did banded foemen destroy thee

Cutting their oxen off, and their flocks so fair, or, it may
     be,
While in a town's defense, or in that of women, con-
     tending?"
     Thus I spake, and he, replying, said to me straight-
     way:
" Nobly-born and wise Odysseus, son of Laertes,
Neither within my ships was I subdued by Poseidon
Rousing the dreadful blast of winds too hard to be mas-
     tered,
Nor on the firm-set land did banded foemen destroy
     me,—
Nay, but death and my doom were well contrived by
     Ægisthos,
Who, with my curséd wife, at his own house bidding me
     welcome,
Fed me, and slew me, as one might slay an ox at the
     manger!
So, by a death most wretched, I died; and all my com-
     panions
Round me were slain off-hand, like white-toothed swine
     that are slaughtered
Thus, when some lordly man, abounding in power and
     riches,
Orders a wedding-feast, or a frolic, or mighty carousal.
Thou indeed hast witnessed the slaughter of numberless
     heroes
Massacred, one by one, in the battle's heat; but with
     pity
All thy heart had been full, if thou hadst seen what I tell
     thee,—
How in the hall we lay among the wine-jars, and under
Tables laden with food; and how the pavement, on all
     sides
Swam with blood! And I heard the dolorous cry of
     Kassandra,

Priam's daughter, whom treacherous Klytæmnestra
    anear me
Slew; and upon the ground I fell in my death-throes,
    vainly
Reaching out hands to my sword, while the shameless
    woman departed,
Nor did she even stay to press her hands on my eyelids,
No, nor to close my mouth, although I was passing to
    Hades.
Oh, there is naught more dire, more insolent than a
    woman
After the very thought of deeds like these has possessed
    her,
One who would dare to devise an act so utterly shame-
    less,
Lying in wait to slay her wedded lord. I bethought me,
Verily, home to my children and servants giving me
    welcome
Safe to return; but she has wrought for herself confusion
Plotting these grievous woes, and for other women here-
    after,
Even for those, in sooth, whose thoughts are set upon
    goodness."
    Thus he spake, and I, in turn replying, addressed him:
" Heavens! how from the first has Zeus the thunderer
    hated,
All for the women's wiles, the brood of Atreus! What
    numbers
Perished in quest of Helen,—and Klytæmnestra, the
    meanwhile,
Wrought in her soul this guile for thee afar on thy jour-
    ney."
    Thus I spake, and he, replying, said to me straightway:
" See that thou art not, then, like me too mild to thy
    helpmeet;
Nor to her ear reveal each secret matter thou knowest,

Tell her the part, forsooth, and see that the rest shall be
     hidden.
Natheless, not unto thee will come such murder, Odys-
     seus,
Dealt by a wife; for wise indeed, and true in her pur-
     pose,
Noble Penelope is, the child of Icarius. Truly,
She it was whom we left, a fair young bride, when we
     started
Off for the wars; and then an infant lay at her bosom,
One who now, methinks, in the list of men must be
     seated,—
Blest indeed! ah, yes, for his well-loved father, returning,
Him shall behold, and the son shall clasp the sire, as is
     fitting.
Not unto me to feast my eyes with the sight of my off-
     spring
Granted the wife of my bosom, but first of life she bereft
     me.
Therefore I say, moreover, and charge thee well to re-
     member,
Unto thine own dear land steer thou thy vessel in secret,
Not in the light; since faith can be placed in woman no
     longer."

Thus ends the Homeric version of Agamemnon's
taking off, and, like everything in Homer, it is the
more impressive for its directness and pathetic simplicity. Granting that the bard, nearly twenty-eight
hundred years ago, was recounting events that occurred two centuries earlier, the dreadful tale would
then have been comparatively fresh tradition and entitled to the force of history.

Four hundred years afterward, Æschylos made the

Attic drama a thing of power and life, affecting the entire range of Greek literature and the sentiment of his people and the State. By this time the simplicity of Homer's history,—or of the Homeric legends, if you choose,—had been superseded. Upon Herbert Spencer's theory of progress a great advance was made —the change from epic plainness to the complexity of the drama, and especially to the abstract impersonations and psychological grandeur of the choric mythology. A still more refined and complex group of ideas came in with Sophokles and Euripides. Whether owing to the lapse of time or to the imagination of these sublime tragedians, the tales of Homer became intermingled with a variety of heroic lore, glossed over with a new dramatic interest and thoroughly infused with a philosophy that was but dimly perceived by the father of epic song. Among the ideas powerfully worked out by Æschylos, and heightening the gloom and glory of his dramas, were those of Tendency governing the history of a person, family, or race; of Nemesis waiting upon crime; of Remorse, and Expiation; finally, of a Destiny to which the Gods themselves must bow. To utilize these, and make them effective elements, he and his compeers took liberties with the record and legends of their country; liberties greater than Shakespeare has taken with the chronicles of Lear, Hamlet, or Macbeth.

The murder of Agamemnon, it is already seen, involved the great accessories of the highest drama, and necessarily became *the leading tragic theme in Greek literature*. It was the royalest chieftain of his age upon whom was wrought this murder, "most foul, strange, and unnatural." In Homer, ambition, guilty love, and jealousy, are the combined motives of the deed. But, to satisfy the wider scope of the dramatists, new forces had to be introduced. The sun is not extinguished by a convulsion that might blot out a star. Nothing but the hand of Destiny, and the implacable Erinnyes, can destroy an Agamemnon. Hence, Æschylos compelled the tragedy of the Atreidæ to date back from the unnatural crime of Atreus himself, who proffered his brother Thyestes the flesh of that brother's son, and who was slain by Thyestes in atonement. The Gods were not forgetful, although permitting Agamemnon to rule in splendor over Argos, and Menelaös to rule over Sparta. Menelaös loses Helena, and the King of Men, at the height of his renown, is murdered by his spouse and her paramour. Here Æschylos also adds, as a human element, the indignation of Klytæmnestra at the death of her daughter, Iphigeneia, decoyed by the King to Aulis under pretense of her marriage to Achilles, and there sacrificed to appease the goddess Artemis. To the king's death succeeds the punishment of the traitorous lovers, who die by the hand of Orestes. The parricide, in turn, is pursued by the Furies, who are appeased only through the intervention of Athena and the Athenians. Finally, the woes and wanderings of Elektra, the sister of Orestes, supply another theme, by turns forceful and tender, to the three tragedians and their differing dramatic modes.

If, among the seven plays of Æschylos remaining

to us, there are one or two valuable for little more
than their illustration of the birth of the Attic drama,
we are compensated by the preservation, not only of
the sublime *Prometheus Desmotes,* but of the three,
intense in human interest, the *Agamemnon, Choëphoroi,* and *Eumenides,* which make the Oresteian
Trilogy complete. It is the one, the priceless trilogy
which has come down from its author and its age.
In *Agamemnon* the King is slain by the direful hand
of Klytæmnestra herself, who then and there became
the typical murderess of all aftertime. The Homeric
story is discarded, and the wife kills her lord as he
emerges from the bath, entangling him first in a gar-
ment as a fish in a net. Leading up to the climax of
the tragedy we have a dialogue, outside the palace,
between the captive Kassandra and the old men of
Argos who compose the chorus. In translation I have,
with few exceptions, followed Paley's text:

[*Æsch., Agam.* 1266-1318.]

CHORUS—KASSANDRA—AGAMEMNON

Chor.—O wretched woman indeed, and O most wise,
       Much hast thou said; but if thou knowest well
       Thy doom, why, like a heifer, by the Gods
       Led to the altar, tread so brave of soul?
Kass.—There's no escape, O friends, the time is full.
Chor.—Natheless, the last to enter gains in time.
Kass.—The day has come; little I make by flight.
Chor.—Thou art bold indeed, and of a daring spirit!
Kass.—Such sayings from the happy none hath heard.
Chor.—Grandly to die is still a grace to mortals.

Kass.—Alas, my Sire,—thee and thy noble brood!
  (*She starts back from the entrance.*)
Chor.—How now? What horror turns thee back again?
Kass.—Faugh! faugh!
Chor.—Why such a cry? There's something chills thy
  soul!
Kass.—The halls breathe murder—ay, they drip with
  blood.
Chor.—How? 'Tis the smell of victims at the hearth.
Kass.—Nay, but the exhalation of the tomb!
Chor.—No Syrian dainty, this, of which thou speakest.
Kass. (*at the portal*)—Yet will I in the palace wail my
    own
  And Agamemnon's fate! Enough of life!
  Alas, O friends!
  Yet not for naught I quail, not as a bird
  Snared in the bush: bear witness, though I die,
  A woman's slaughter shall requite my own,
  And, for this man ill-yoked a man shall fall!
  Thus prays of you a stranger, at death's door.
Chor.—Lost one, I rue with thee thy foretold doom!
Kass.—Once more I fain would utter words, once more,—
  'Tis my own threne! And I invoke the Sun,
  By his last beam, that my detested foes
  May pay no less to them who shall avenge me,
  Than I who die an unresisting slave!

               *   *   *   *   *

                (*She enters the palace.*)
Chor.—Of Fortune was never yet enow
  To mortal man; and no one ever
  Her presence from his house would sever
  And point, and say, " Come no more nigh! "
  Unto our King granted the Gods on high
        That Priam's towers should bow,
  And homeward, crowned of Heaven, hath he come;
  But now if, for the ancestral blood that lay

                    [241]

At his doors, he falls,—and the dead, that cursed his
home,
    He, dying, must in full requite,—
What manner of man is one that would not pray
    To be born with a good attendant Sprite?
    (*An outcry within the palace.*)

Agamemnon.—Woe's me! I am stricken a deadly blow
within!

Chor.—Hark! Who is't cries "a blow"? Who meets
his death?

Agam.—Woe's me! again! a second time I am stricken!

Chor.—The deed, methinks, from the King's cry, is done.
    Quick, let us see what help may be in counsel!

Whereupon the old men, one by one, make some
terror-stricken and absurd remarks, which only serve
to fill out the time until the royal murderess can enter
upon the scene. The poet evidently conceives her as
a stately and defiant woman, despising the clamor of
the throng, while she stands full height in the palace
door, still holding the bloody weapon in her hands:

[*Agam.* 1343-1377.]

Enter KLYTÆMNESTRA, *from the Palace.*

Klyt.—Now, all this formal outcry having vent,
I shall not blush to speak the opposite.
How should one, plotting evil things for foes,
Encompass seeming friends with such a bane
Of toils? it were a height too great to leap!
Not without full prevision came, though late,
To me this crisis of an ancient feud.
And here, the deed being done, I stand—even where
I smote him! nor deny that thus I did it;

[242]

So that he could not flee nor ward off doom.
A seamless net, as round a fish, I cast
About him, yea, a deadly wealth of robe;
Then smote him twice; and with a double cry
He loosed his limbs; and to him fallen I gave
Yet a third thrust, a grace to Hades, lord
Of the underworld and guardian of the dead.
So, falling, out he gasps his soul, and out
He spurts a sudden jet of blood, that smites
Me with a sable rain of gory dew,—
Me, then no less exulting than the field
In the sky's gift, while bursts the pregnant ear!
Things being thus, old men of Argos, joy,
If joy ye can;—I glory in the deed!
And if 'twere seemly ever yet to pour
Libation to the dead, 'twere most so now;
Most meet that one, who poured for his own home
A cup of ills, returning, thus should drain it!

Chor.—Shame on thy tongue! how bold of mouth thou art
That vauntest such a speech above thy husband!

Klyt.—Ye try me as a woman loose of soul;
But I with dauntless heart avow to you
Well knowing—and whether ye choose to praise or
blame
I care not—this is Agamemnon; yea,
My husband; yea, a corpse, of this right hand,
This craftsman sure, the handiwork! Thus stands it.

The third thrust, given by the Queen, to make the
murder sure, or, as she puts it, " as a votive offering
to Hades," is an act in strong contrast to the timorous
course pursued by the Klytæmnestra of Homer—who
has not wholly unsexed herself, but flees in terror
from the corpse-strewn banquet hall. Æschylos drew
the prototype of Lady Macbeth, and nothing equal to

the foregoing speech appeared again in literature until
Shakespeare wrote:

> Infirm of purpose!
> Give me the daggers: the sleeping and the dead
> Are but as pictures: 'tis the eye of childhood
> That fears a painted devil. * * * *
> My hands are of your color; but I shame
> To wear a heart so white!

I will omit the greater portion of the choruses and
dialogue which follow the Queen's avowal, but translate a few of the strophes and antistrophes alluding
to the evil auspices of the Atreidæ and to the sacrifice
of Iphigeneia:

[*Agam.* 1466-1507.]

CHORUS—SEMI-CHORUS—KLYTÆMNESTRA

Chorus.   Woe! Woe!
   King! O how shall I weep for thy dying?
     What shall my fond heart say anew?
   Thou in the web of the spider art lying,
     Breathing out life by a death she shall rue!
Semi-Chorus.—Alas! alas for this slavish couch! By a
     sword
   Two-edged, by a hand untrue,
   Thou art smitten, even to death, my lord!
Klyt.—Thou sayest this deed was mine alone;
     But I bid thee call me not
   The wife of Agamemnon's bed;
   'Twas the ancient fell Alastor [1] of Atreus' throne,

[1] The Evil Genius, the Avenger.

[244]

The lord of a horrid feast, this crime begot,
Taking a shape that seemed the wife of the dead,—
  His sure revenge, I wot,
A victim ripe hath claimed for the young that bled.
Semi-Chorus.—Who shall bear witness now,—
Who of this murder, now, thee guiltless hold?
      How sayest thou? How?
Yet the fell Alastor may have holpen, I trow:
    Still is dark Ares driven
    Down currents manifold
Of kindred blood, wherever judgment is given,
And he comes to avenge the children slain of old,
  And their thick gore cries to Heaven!
Chorus.   Woe! Woe!
  King! O how shall I weep for thy dying?
  What shall my fond heart say anew?
  Thou in the web of the spider art lying,
    Breathing out life by a death she shall rue!

Semi-Chorus.—Alas! alas for this slavish couch! By a
    sword
  Two-edged, by a hand untrue,
Thou art smitten, even to death, my lord!

Klyt.—Hath he not subtle Atè brought
      Himself, to his kingly halls?
  'Twas on our own dear offspring,—yea,
On Iphigeneia, wept for still, he wrought
The doom that cried for the doom by which he falls.
O, let him not in Hades boast, I say,
    For 'tis the sword that calls,
Even for that foul deed, his soul away!

A volume might still be written upon the strength
and beauty of the Agamemnon of Æschylos. But for
the purpose of this sketch no supplement is needed to

the masterly criticism of Schlegel and Müller, or to the verdict of poets and men of letters from the earliest time. Kassandra having shared, as she had predicted, the fate of her master, the doors are opened, and Klytæmnestra and Ægisthos, with loving words to each other and defiance to the populace, retain possession of the kingdom. In the remaining portions of the Trilogy, one woe doth tread upon another's heel. The *Choëphoroi* recounts the vengeance of Orestes, who finds his sister offering libations at their father's tomb, disguises himself, and finally slays his mother and her paramour. In the *Eumenides*, haunted by the ghost of Klytæmnestra, and lashed by the Furies, he goes to Delphi and Athens for trial and expiation. These dramas are second in importance only to the *Agamemnon*, and afford vivid illustrations of the poet's affection for Athens, and of the greatness of that city in his own time as the centre of culture and power.

Only one of Sophokles' plays is devoted to the theme before us. With his special refinement, and tenderness for woman, he made Elektra its heroine, and analyzed her feelings and experience. This drama, like the *Choëphoroi*, narrates the punishment of the Queen by Orestes; but here the accepted legends were changed again to suit the genius of the poet. As for Euripides, it is not strange that, after the theme had been already used by his great masters, he should have made a failure with his own *Elektra*. In *Orestes* he was more successful, as far as tragic power is concerned, but the piece is involved and burdened with extraneous incident. In *Iphigeneia in Aulis* and *Iphigeneia in Tauris* he discovered a field and heroine of his own, and, especially in the former play, earns his right to be called " Euripides, the Human," and justifies the lines of Browning:

Euripides
Last the old hand on the old phorminx flung,
*   *   *   *   *   *   *
Then music sighed itself away; one moan
Iphigeneia made by Aulis' strand;
With her and music died Euripides.

Without looking beyond the epic and dramatic poets, it is seen that the story of the woes of the House of Atreus assumes the foremost position as a theme for the daring efforts of the great masters of antique song. It also has been more deeply wrought into the heart and structure of general literature than any other tale of olden time. It has been cited and utilized by sages, historians, romancers, throughout the centuries even to the present day. The killing of Agamemnon became the ideal murder of imaginative literature, the standard from which all others take their measure; more truly so than that of Abel by Cain, because it involves a larger association of human motives, revenges, expiations. It has been treated in a hundred modes, from the primitive and serious chronicle of Homer to the charade enacted by Colonel and Mrs. Rawdon Crawley (the latter " quite killing in the part ") before the noble guests of my lord, the Marquis of Steyne.

[247]

What historical bearing, then, has the news thus far received from Dr. Schliemann upon the tradition whose literary significance we have been examining? In the least hopeful view—should no unmistakable symbols, or other record, come to light—the discoveries already made, taken in connection with the results attained in the Troad, will greatly strengthen our faith in the historic value of enduring song. In those who have always thought of Agamemnon as a hero of pure fiction, it will breed a disposition to consider him a veritable personage, who ruled and died in Argos, and the catastrophe of whose death was somewhat as stated in the Odyssey.

Little in classic story goes behind the fall of Troy. Agamemnon and Helena are of the celestial breed. Another generation and you come to the demigods; one more, and to the Gods themselves. All this is precisely on a level with the tradition of other peoples, as they have reached the Homeric plane of enlightenment. The same in Assyria, the same in Phœnicia, in Egypt, in Peru and Mexico of the Western World. Less than four centuries ago an Homeric civilization was found and overwhelmed by Cortez and Pizarro. Allow for the inferior quality of the darker races, scarcely capable, if time had been given, of a much higher development, and how closely analogous the civilization of the Aztecs to that of the Homeric chiefs! Colossal architecture, wealth of silver and gold and the products of the loom, superstition, priests and soothsayers, royal demigods, altars for human sacrifices, the latter more frequent and more sanguinary in the New World than in the Old. All this blotted out in a recent period, and yet before Science had arisen to properly analyze and perpetuate its record. And now the whole round world is known to us; and now, the round world over, the Trojan ages are forever past.

XX

SIDNEY LANIER [1]

CERTAINLY all who care for whatsoever things are pure, lovely, and of good report, must be deeply concerned in the record and ending of Lanier's earthly pilgrimage; concerned no less, if ever they chanced to meet him, in the mingled softness and strength of his nature, the loyalty with which he sang his song, pursued his researches, and took the failures and successes of his consecrated life. For, if there ever was a pilgrim who bore a vow, or a life consecrate to an ideal, such a votary was this poet-artist, and so manifestly ordered was his too-brief life.

You will speak to one another of his brave spirit, of the illness and trials that handicapped him, and of the cheerful industry with which he went through daily tasks, and yet so often escaped to the region of poetry and art. That he had the graceful and practical talent that can adapt itself to use, and give pleasure to the simplest minds, was proved by his admirable books for the young, and the professional labors fresh in your recollection. But in the mould of Lanier, as in that of every real poet, the imaginative qualities and the

[1] A letter to President Gilman, of Johns Hopkins University, read at the Memorial Gathering to Sidney Lanier. *The Critic,* November 5, 1881.

sense of beauty governed and gave tone to all other senses and motive powers. He was first of all a poet and artist, and of a refined and novel order.

No man, in fact, displayed more clearly the poetic and artistic temperaments in their extreme conjunction. It may be said that they impeded, rather than hastened, his power of adequate expression. He strove to create a new language for their utterance, and a method of his own. To reach the effects toward which his subtle instincts guided him, he required a prolonged lifetime of experiment and discovery; and to him how short a life was given—and that how full of impediment! He had scarcely sounded the key-note of his overture when the bow fell from his hand; and beyond all this he meant to compose, not an air or a tune, but a symphony—one involving all harmonic resources, and combinations before unknown.

I find that I am involuntarily using the diction of music to express the purpose of his verse, and this fact alone has a bearing upon what he did, and what he did not do, as an American poet. What seemed affectation in him was his veritable nature, which differed from, and went beyond, or outside, that of other men. He gave us now and then some lyric, wandering or regular, that was marked by sufficient beauty, pathos, weirdness, to show what he might have accomplished, had he been content to sing spontaneously— as very great poets have sung—without analyzing his processes till the song was done. But Lanier was a musician, and still heard in his soul "the music of wondrous melodies." He had, too, the constructive

mind of the artist who comprehends the laws of form
and tone. How logical was his exposition of the
mathematics of beauty is seen in that unique work,
The Science of English Verse.

Now it is a question whether, Art being so long,
and Time so fleeting, a poet should consider too anx-
iously the rationale of his song. Again, he strove to
demonstrate in his verse the absolute co-relations of
music and poetry—and seemed at times to forget that
rhythm is but one component of poetry, albeit one most
essential. While music is one of the poet's servitors,
and must ever be compelled to his use, there still remains that boundary of Lessing's between the liberties
of the two arts, though herein less sharply defined than
between those of poetry and painting. The rhythm
alone of Lanier's verse often had a meaning to himself
that others found it hard to understand. Of this he
was conscious. In a letter to me, he said that one
reason for his writing *The Science of English Verse*
was, that he had some poems which he hoped
soon to print, but which "he could not hope to get
understood, generally, without educating their audience." To this he added that the task was "inexpressi-
bly irksome" to him, and that he "never could have
found courage to endure it save for the fact that in
all directions the poetic art was suffering from the
shameful circumstance that criticism was without a
scientific basis for even the most elementary of its
judgments."

If, in dwelling upon the science of his art, he hampered the exercise of it, he was none the less a man

of imagination, of ideality; none the less, at first sight, in bearing, features, conversation, a poet and lover of the beautiful. His name is added to the names of those whose haunting strain

> Ends incomplete, while through the starry night,
> The ear still waits for what it did not tell.

Yet the sense of incompleteness and of regret for his broken life is tempered by the remembrance that the most suggestive careers of poets have not always been those which were fully rounded, but often of those whose voices reach us from early stages of the march which it was not given them long to continue.

XXI

JULIA WARD HOWE [1]

MRS. HOWE long since won from the popular heart a tribute, rendered to her ardent human sympathies, her inborn love of freedom, and her patriotism, sustained and unfaltering through the nation's darkest hour. The critics also have delighted to honor one who looks in her heart and writes; and whose writings, though woman-like utterances of inner life and thought, have little subjectivity of a morbid or sentimental kind.

A poet of such achievements and intent has passed beyond the period of gentle appreciation and tender, nursing regard. She has earned the right to fair and independent criticism. We may now estimate her merits and defects. If she has left undone those things which she ought to have done, they who tell her so will, perhaps, inspire her with motives for new and better methods in her chosen work.

It is thought that in music, literature, the arts of painting and sculpture, as well as in all mechanical processes, women, with their swift, natural facility, arrive at a certain excellence much more rapidly than men, but that beyond this point they often lack the

[1] *The Round Table,* February 3, 1866.

patience or faculty to proceed; while their brothers
always feel some inward sense impelling them to
greater mastery of their professions. The foremost
men are those who include woman's intuition with
their own strengthening purpose; the noblest women
acquire a masculine conscientiousness of treatment in
whatever work they undertake. Has Mrs. Howe thus
enhanced her womanly endowments? Between her
Passion Flowers, published in 1854, and these
Later Lyrics, we fail to discover much artistic advance or gain in intellectual clearness. The former
volume was noticeable for great merits and great
faults; but the faults are equally conspicuous, if not
exaggerated, in the collection under review.

What is Mrs. Howe's standard of excellence? Let
us repeat it from her own lips. The first among her
Poems of Study and Experience reveals it plainly,
and is, we observe, one of the most incisive and
finished pieces in the volume:

TO THE CRITIC

Of all my verses, say that one is good,
So shalt thou give more praise than Hope might claim;
And from my poet-grave, to vex thy soul,
No ghost shall rise, whose deeds demand a name.

A thousand loves, and only one shall stand
To show us what its counterfeits should be;
The blossoms of a spring-tide, and but one
Bears the world's fruit—the seed of History.

A thousand rhymes shall pass, and only one
Show, crystal-shod, the Muse's twinkling feet;

A thousand pearls the haughty Ethiop spurned
Ere one could make her luxury complete.

In goodliest palaces, some meanest room
The owner's smallness shields contentedly.
Nay, further; of the manifold we are,
But one pin's point shall pass eternity.

Exalt, then, to the greatness of the throne
One only of these beggarlings of mine;
I with the rest will dwell in modest bounds:
The chosen one shall glorify the line.

If the singer will stand by her pledge, we may sleep
sound of nights, with no spectral visitations. Not
one, but many, are her verses which we pronounce to
be good, enjoy as such, and are thankful for. Of
Poems of the War, those entitled "Our Orders,"
"Left Behind," "The Battle Eucharist," are rapturous expressions of the abnegation, the exaltation, and
the deep religious faith which carried our people
through the recent contest. "The Battle Hymn of
the Republic," with its profound Hebraic spirit, and
wrathful, exultant swell, seems, verily, to have borne
"the world's fruit—the seed of history." The first
of the "Parables" is a simple and tender rendering of
the text, "Inasmuch as ye did it not to one of the
least of these, ye did it not to me." The series of
love poems entitled "Her Verses" are sensuous, if
not simple, and have truer passion in them than can
be found in other lyrics depending upon interjectional
outbursts for their effect. But in some of the *Poems
of Study and Experience,* Mrs. Howe seems to be

raised, by higher thought, to higher art, and more nearly achieves success. " Philosophy and First Causes," and " The Christ " will repay any one's reading. " The Church " is in harmony with the free and catholic spirit of its author. Our attention is next caught by a little madrigal, called " The Evening Ride," which we quote as having *musical quality,* and being, therefore, one of the few pieces that can justly come under the title of this book:

> Through purple clouds with golden crests
> I go to find my lover;
> Hid from my sight this many a year,
> My heart must him discover:
> I know the lair of the timid hare,
> The nest of the startled plover.
>
> O earth! of all thy garlands, keep
> The fairest for our meeting;
> Could we ask music, 'twere to drown
> The heart's tumultuous beating,
> That only eyes, in glad surprise,
> Might look through tears their greeting.
>
> If Time have writ my beauty out,
> I have no charm to bind him;
> No snare to catch his doubting soul,
> Nor vow exchanged to bind him;
> But this I keep, that I must weep
> Bitterly when I find him.

The reader will also admire " Simple Tales," " Fame and Friendship," " Meditation," " The House of Rest," and other thoughtful poems. " The Unwelcome Message " is very striking, having much of the solemn quality which so impresses one in the " Up-Hill " of Christina Rossetti; but the latter artist would never have ruined her effect by toning up the closing stanza with commonplace light. To us, however, it seems that the most emotional and sweetest passages of the book are to be found in the poems on an infant's life and death—" The Babe's Lesson," " Spring Blossoms," " Remembrance," and especially the verses entitled " Little One." Whoever reads the latter will see what Mrs. Howe can do when feeling carries away the obscure vapors which often becloud her art.

Having thus exempted ourselves from reproach, under the rule made in " Lines to the Critic," we now proceed, lawyer-like—but in no pettifogging spirit—to take exception to the sentiment which those lines avow.

We hold that only a poor and unworthy purpose is content to throw off verse after verse, in the hope that one out of many will have poetic value. As well might a sculptor make rude, distorted figures, content with now and then conforming an image to the beauty of nature and finishing it to the fingers' ends. Is not a poem as truly a work of art as a statue or a painting, and are not all arts one in completeness? The safe, the noble rule is *never* to write a bad poem. We do not hold that this standard can be maintained; yet, in our day, several have come very near it. There are living poets (and poets who will live), each of whose pieces has such merit that we know not how to spare anything they have produced. If they have made poor verses, it has been in silence, and the manuscripts have been ignominiously crumpled, like Beau Brummell's " failures " in cravats. Why print anything that can be omitted—that is not a positive addition to literature? Of course, we all do this continually, but to do it avowedly, to do it " on principle " —that is, indeed, malice aforethought! Now, of the hundred and odd lyrics in Mrs. Howe's book there are fifty—we do not say devoid of poetry, but whose omission would benefit the author's reputation; and of the remainder, how few there are which are conscientiously finished, and, therefore, up to the requirements of the time!

The time, we say, has requirements equally binding with those of hope and patriotism. Loyalty to country and one's race will not alone suffice; there is a loyalty to art, our sovereign mistress, our early and eternal desire. In the age of chivalry there were Courts of Love, where coquettes and unfaithful suitors were indicted; and we do now cite this author into the High Court of Art, and, in gentle terms, impeach her of certain malfeasance. She shall be her own judge on the evidence adduced, and, if conviction ensue, will, perchance, hold herself in bonds for the more faithful performance of her high mission.

A feature of Mrs. Howe's verses, as of Mrs. Browning's, is their earnestness; but this becomes too often a coarse defect. It is revealed in spasmodic utterance, or in words big and painful with a meaning that will not out, and ejaculations of the Gerald-

Massey order—is rhetorical, eloquent, gushing, anything but lyrical and poetic. Mrs. Browning's impulses led her continually on the same path; but noble imagination lifted her lightly above the wildwood thicket in which she went astray, and her sacred fire seemed to consume the brambles clinging to her skirts. Mrs. Howe's genius is not sufficient to redeem her teacher's faults, and the latter she has copied to excess. She seems to write before her idea is thoroughly defined to herself. The result is a confused imagery, and language strangely involved. Her obscurity is not that of thought too elevated for expression in words, for clear thoughts find the highest and purest utterance. It is rather the outward symbol of imperfect inner sight, and leads her into bewildering inversions, ignoble conceits, inelegant and even ungrammatical forms. We cite a few instances of what we mean:

> Lost on the turbid current of the street,
>   My *pearl doth swim;*
> Oh, for the diver's cunning hands and feet
>   To come to *him!*

> And only the sun's warm fire
>   Stirs softly *their* happy *breast.*

> Ye harmless household drudges,
>   Your draggled *daily wear,*
> And *horny palms* of labor,
>   A softer heart may *bear.*

> Death's cold purity condense
> Vaporous sin to soul's intense.

Life ye tear to shred and flitter,
Joying in the costly glitter
To rehearse each art-abortion
That consumes a widow's portion.

The skies have left one *marble drop*
Within the *lily's heart*.

Here is a stanza that can only find its counterpart in Sternhold and Hopkins's version of the Psalms:

The murderer's wicked lust
Their righteous steps withstood:
The zeal that thieves and pirates knew
Brought down the guiltless blood.

Mrs. Howe invariably says Jèsu for Jesus; and her prayer is always an Ave. Among her crippled and unscholarly devices of expression are such words and phrases as " sweat-embossed," " sense-magic," " weird-encircled," " inmould," " poor occurrence," " recondite dinners," " man's idle irk," " love's eterne," " solvent skies," " in wondrous sequency involved," " life's great impersonate," " prince's minivère," and so forth, since these are taken at random from a barbaric host. She tells us of one who " passions with her glance," and elsewhere bids " dawn's sentinels " to " shed golden balsam." Who else could have written such a stanza as this?

Deep Night, within thy gloomy catafalque
Bury my grief;
And, while thy candles light my funeral walk,
Promise relief.

The faulty rhyme in this stanza is the least of its offences, but suggests others which have kept us in a stumbling and apprehensive condition throughout our reading of these lyrics:

" Rule—full," " shady—ready," " daily—railway," " God—bowed," " host—lost," " attracts-us—backs-us," " fingers—singers," " rudeness—voidness," " joy—by," " coin—shine," " kindred—hundred," " teeth—death," " grieve—shrive," etc.

Mrs. Howe wisely clings to quatrains in which only the second and fourth lines are paired, and if she would follow Mr. Walt Whitman's ingenious system, casting rhyme (no less than metre) beneath her feet, she would at least show it more consideration than in couplets with such endings as these. This may be technical criticism, but is not on a minor matter. The great poets know better than to do these things. A vile rhyme breaks in upon the full-flowing river of written song as rudely as a flat note upon the aria of a prima donna. It is, like dropping the ring at a wedding, a shock and an evil omen. But Mrs. Howe's carelessness in this regard is merely a part of the system by which she utters equally disjointed thought. There can be nothing more odd than the constant juxtaposition of vigorous and feeble verses in her poems. The third and fourth stanzas addressed " To the Critic " furnish an example. More frequently, however, she will commence a lyric with a really fine verse, and let the reader down so woefully before the close that he begins to ask himself whether anti-climax is not her favorite figure of speech.

If these shortcomings arise from constitutional disability—from natural lack of power to express—they present serious arguments against a verdict that Mrs. Howe is a poet. She may be full of poetic feeling, appreciative and reflective, may possess the undoubted poetical temperament; but poetical power consists in the *faculty of utterance,* and the poet is not only a seer, but a " maker "—a revealer of what he sees. If they come from impatience of revision, or too great devotion to that social life in which Mrs. Howe cannot fail to be an honor and a charm, they may and will be amended, if she will be conscientious and true to her art-career. If they are due to the ready praises of undiscriminating friends, we would rather not rank among the number of those who thus take away from a gifted aspirant more than they can possibly bestow. What we have thought is written in a sincere and, we trust, not ungenerous spirit. And if Mrs. Howe will study more closely those masters of English song whose manner is furthest removed from that which has hitherto most guided her; if she will add to the fire and humanity of her lyrics the harmonies of order, the grace of completeness, and the strength of repose, our voice shall be among the foremost to claim for her the Sapphic crown.

XXII

EMMA LAZARUS[1]

WHILE thoroughly feminine, and a mistress of the social art and charm, she was—though without the slighest trace of pedantry—the natural companion of scholars and thinkers. Her emotional nature kept pace with her intellect; as she grew in learning and mental power, she became still more earnest, devoted, impassioned.

These advances marked her writings—especially her poetry, which changed in later years from its early reflection of the Grecian ideals and took on a lyrical and veritably Hebraic fire and imagination. You have rightly said of her that ' she wrote only when inspired '; and there was a contagious inspiration in her Semitic ardor, her satire, wrath and exaltation. That she was able to impart these qualities to sustained creative work is shown by her strangely powerful drama ' The Dance to Death,' unique in American poetry. Viewed merely on the literary side, her abilities were so progressive, under the quickening force of a lofty motive, that her early death is a deplorable loss in a time when so much verse, if not as sounding brass, seems to come from tinkling cymbals.

[1] A letter read at the exercises in commemoration of the life and work of Emma Lazarus, 1905.

During the last few years, owing to her change of residence, I met Miss Lazarus less frequently, and I scarcely knew what inference to derive from your feeling biographical sketch, as to her religious attitude and convictions. That she was aglow with the Jewish spirit, proud of her race's history and characteristics, and consecrated to its freedom from oppression throughout the world,—all this is finely manifest; yet her intellectual outlook was so broad that I took her to be a modern Theist in religion, and one who would not stipulate for absolute maintenance of the barriers with which the Mosaic law isolated the Jewish race, in certain respects, from the rest of mankind. Taking into account, however, the forces of birth and training, I could understand how our Miriam of to-day, filled with the passion of her cause, should return to the Pentateuchal faith—to the Mosaic ritual in its hereditary and most uncompromising form. Nor would any lover of the heroic in life or literature, if such had been her course, desire to have it otherwise.

Eighteen years have passed since I wrote the foregoing characterization, under the grave sense of loss inspired by the pity of her death at the very bloom of her creative genius and her new aspiration.

I saw Miss Lazarus most frequently between 1879 and 1881, when our homes were not far apart and she was often an admired guest in my household. One evening she confided to me her feeling of despondency as to her poetic work; a belief that, with all her passion for. beauty and justice, she " had accomplished nothing to stir, nothing to awaken, to teach or to suggest, nothing that the world could not equally well do without." These very words I take from a letter received from her in the same week, and they are the substance of what she had spoken. Although no American poet of her years had displayed from childhood a more genuine gift than hers, I knew exactly what she meant. She had followed art for art's sake, along classic lines, and had added no distinctive element to English song. It suddenly occurred to me to ask her why she had been so indifferent to a vantage-ground which she, a Jewess of the purest stock, held above any other writer. Persecutions of her race were then beginning in Europe. She said that, although proud of her blood and lineage, the Hebrew ideals did not appeal to her; but I replied that I envied her the inspiration she might derive from them.

It was not long before outrages to which the Jews were subjected in Eastern and middle Europe began to stir the civilized world, and the heart and spirit of Emma Lazarus thrilled, as I from the first had believed they would, with the passion and indignation that supplied the motive needed for her song. When we were electrified by those glowing lyrics, " The Crowing of the Red Cock," and " The Banner of the Jew," I felt that she at last had come to her own. When she died, a princess was fallen in Israel. Would that her hand were here to smite the harp, in this hour of her race's supreme and last ordeal in the Old World, and equally to sound the note of jubilation and prophecy as you celebrate, even now, the settlement of your historic people upon a continent where no tyranny checks their freedom and progress.

XXIII

KIPLING'S BALLADS OF "THE SEVEN SEAS"[1]

THE dedication of Mr. Kipling's new collection of ballads is a significant poem, "To the City of Bombay," his birthplace.

> Between the palms and the sea,
> Where the world-end steamers wait.

This, like the prelude to his earlier book of verse, avows a recognition of the forces that have had most to do with his work. He finds it well that his birth fell not in "waste headlands of the earth"; but the world sees also that no more fortunate chance could befall an Englishman of his generation, and of a genius that would be manifest in any environment, than to be born in a distant and imperial British dependency; to be bred to realize what has made his nation so great; and thus, of all English writers, best to know the hearts of "such as fought and sailed and ruled and loved and made our world."

This good fortune, if through it he has lost something of the idyllic charm and sweetness, has saved

[1] *The Book Buyer,* November, 1896.

him from the over-refinement which glosses the exquisite measures in which England's home-keeping
poets give us chiefly variations of thoughts and themes
essentially the same. The faultless verse of the closing period surely needed a corrective. The breath of
Kipling's fresh and virile song swept across it like
a channel sea-wind driving the spindrift over hedge
and garden-close. Both its spirit and its method have
taken the English-reading world, and they maintain
their hold in this new collection, entitled *The Seven
Seas*.

Few authors comprehend so well their natural bent
as Mr. Kipling, or have the sense to follow it so
bravely. At this stage, and as a poet, he is a balladist
through and through, though one likely enough to be
eminent in any effort which he may seriously undertake. The balladist's gift is distinctive. A single
lyric of Drayton's, the thousandth part of his work,
has made his name heroic. Browning's "Hervé
Riel" and Tennyson's "The Revenge" and "Luck-
now" show that their authors returned to the ballad,
and not to something less, at the very height of their
fame. We feel that, as a balladist alone, the preacher-
poet of the "Last Buccaneer" and "Lorraine" was
near of kin to his greater compeers, and if Thornbury's
stars had not destined him to be a hack-writer, the
Songs of the Cavaliers and Roundheads would not
now be out of print through the obscurity of his name.
But the splendor of "The English Flag" and "The
Ballad of East and West," and the originality and
weird power of "Danny Deever," find in the present

volume and its predecessor a score of counterparts almost as striking, and find their foil, it must be added, in pieces quite below Kipling's level and really harmful to his fame. As he may fairly consider himself still near the outset of his career, one may hope that the latter class will in time be banished from collective editions of his poetry, and that no literary ghoul of the future will venture to restore them.

Genius is said to be proved by its lapses, but even genius, since Tennyson, has been usually " successful " in technique. Kipling, however, with his fine reliance upon the first intention, never emasculates his verse; on the other hand, either through a lack of self-restraint, or working too often for a tempting wage, he achieves more failures than are needed to distinguish his gift from talent by the negative test. These are not wanting in the new barrack-room ballads. What is best in them is scarcely new, and what is new is not indispensable. " Back to the Army Again," " Soldier and Sailor Too," and perhaps a third or fourth, may well go with the " Tommy " and " Fuzzy-Wuzzy " of old, but one can spare a dozen others which seem but " runnin' emptyings " of the Atkins beer. It needs the British private at his best to make us tolerate the " Gawd " and " bloomin' " lingo that only heroism and our poet's magic can ennoble. Not a little of Kipling's balladry is also in a sense too esoteric. The life of this most primitive and spontaneous form of poetry is simplicity. True, there is one simplicity for the elect, and another for the multitude, but there must be something in a strong work that appeals to all. The realism of a lyric, moreover, be it cockney slang or other detail, must interest the future no less than the present, the ultimate test being endurance. These reflections would not be worth while in the case of a lesser man. Mr. Kipling now can afford to be silent for long intervals, rather than to give out a single stanza that is not in his happier vein.

But while dainty rhymesters hoard and pare, the public will never contemn so resourceful and generous a lyrical spendthrift. When we turn to the larger portion of *The Seven Seas,* how imaginative it is, how impassioned, how superbly rhythmic and sonorous! Kipling now betakes himself to the main which English keels have ploughed for ages, and, like them, makes it his own from the tropics to the pole. "A Song of the English," with its ballads and interludes, is the cantata of a master. "The Rhyme of the Three Sealers" is grimly intrepid—his ruthless Yankee skippers are transformed to Vikings in the arctic fog. "The Mary Gloster" and "McAndrew's Hymn" are, each in its way, thoroughly realistic—the latter monologue being as true a comprehension of the ingrained Scottish temper as can be drawn—stronger, in fact, than most of Browning's dramatic monologues when he left the middle ages for a contemporary study of that kind. "The Song of the Banjo," with its masterly refrains, is resonant of pathos, humor, and the world-around music of vagrants that, when all is said, are the world's pioneers. And of these ballads the most remarkable is that

rollicking unique, " The Last Chantey," doubtless one
of the purest examples, since Coleridge's wondrous
" Rime," of the imaginatively grotesque. That it *is*
a grotesque may exile it from the highest field of art,
but, like Doré's masterpiece, *Le Juif Errant,* it is
a paragon of its kind. It is true to the mental cos-
mology of the sailor class, and to the author's own
fancy (as seen in " Tomlinson " and the Prelude to
the earlier Ballads) by its retention of the mediæval
notion of God, the Devil, and supramundane goings-on
—as much so as the overture of *Faust.* The measure is roysteringly delightful. Who but Kipling would
take up the catch of " All round my hat I vears a
green villow," and use it for a ballad which, if fantastic, is of magnificent grade? Such an expedient,
that few would detect, shows that his methods are as
bold as his imaginings, and that no good workman
need be at a loss for tools.

The ring and diction of all this verse add new elements to our song. Kipling's realism proves again
that the strongest flights are taken from the ground
of truth—that ideality and experience are not antag-
onistic. More than other modern poets of England,
he has had the liberty of her realm; for him sea and
shore, ice and desert-sand, are Britain's domain, or
that of those who speak her tongue. Of such, the
soldier and sailor, the explorer, of every degree, are
his people, and the traders large and small. To reveal their sensations is easy for the insight that created a demonic soul within the Ganges " Mugger "
and is on human terms with all the beasts of the jungle.

Kipling's national mode of thought found expression in the proud outburst, " What should they know of England who only England know!" He is now more than ever the celebrant of the empire, and of the deeds of men that extend it:

> If blood be the price of Admiralty,
> Lord God we ha' paid it in!

He is thus, in some degree, the true laureate of Greater Britain. Others may sing the praise of a home administration, but his song is scornful of form and rule that irk or fail to comprehend the English spirit in its courses round the globe. Of all Victorian poets Tennyson was the most indubitably an Englishman, from a focal and outlooking point of view; and among those that survive, Kipling expresses the imperial inspiration, from every far-off station which he knows so well, looking toward the central isles. It is impossible that America, boding the unwritten federation of English-speaking peoples, should not be on closer terms with Mr. Kipling than with other transatlantic singers, by virtue of whatever share we still possess in the greatness of our ancient motherland.

XXIV

WENDELL'S "COTTON MATHER"[1]

FOR the sub-title of this book, "The Puritan Priest," doubtless many readers would think "The Puritan Prelate" might be substituted,—so well established have become our traditions of the most renowned of the Mathers: traditions perhaps strengthened, since the appearance of Tyler's *American Literature,* by its author's vivid alignment of the Mather Dynasty. But this new and faithful examination of a stormy, self-torturing career makes it evident that priest and not prelate is the fit appellative. Dr. Cotton Mather, though in temper the most autocratic of his race, held no undisputed sway. His proud and armored spirit, humbling itself to none save Jehovah,—self-elected to be His familiar, even as Abraham and Moses had been of old,—found barriers that pent it in, and against which it beat in vain. It was freest and most potent in his early prime, while his father Increase was also at the height of influence. Apparently from the day when, in the flush of youth and denunciatory zeal, he strode his horse and harangued an awe-stricken throng at the hanging of George Burroughs on Salem hill, both his secular

[1] *The Critic,* January 2, 1892.

[274]

authority and his power to maintain the stern Hebraic law and ritual in the Old Colony grew less and less. To the end of his life he found himself more or less a suspect, criticised, hampered, gainsayed, by the laity and his sacerdotal peers; slowly but surely, to his grief and bewilderment, getting farther away from his inherited rights as the chief exponent of the ancestral creed and New England's spiritual potentate.

He found himself, while keenly alive to his prerogatives as the flower of theocratic generations, lacking real advancement; forced, after all, to take refuge in his learning, subtlety, mysticism, and in what Professor Wendell analyzes as the " histrionic insincerity of priesthood that brings to unhappy men the Divine sympathy of priests." One soon discovers that Mr. Wendell is a master of paradoxy: it is his natural method of getting at a radical truth. In using it for honest needs, rather than for effect, he is original and gives his style a decidedly specific flavor.

Dr. Mather, then, even in that colonial period, was an anachronism. He incurred the obloquy of many who advanced beyond his creed, and in whom his vanity and egregious manner bred a hearty antagonism. And he died after experience of foiled ambitions, grievously baffled, it is clear, in never securing the Presidency of Harvard—which his father held for sixteen years. He saw that college dangerously liberalized, and was driven to strengthen Yale as the citadel of the true faith, where a glorious defence could still be made—the outposts having been sapped if not taken. Yale College—how would the Doctor esti-

mate her now?—can never forget that to Cotton
Mather's influence she owed a helpful endowment and
a name.   Meanwhile, after every rebuff and humilia-
tion, and in the domestic tragedies that shrouded his
later years, he went to his closet like the men of old,
and wrestled with his Puritan God. He invariably
restored his wounded self-respect by comforting en-
tries in the diaries begun in youth and assiduously
kept up—despite the labor of writing some hundreds
of other volumes—throughout his life. To an acquaintance with his pangs and ecstasies we are skilfully led by the present biographer. We enter into
his secret thoughts; we know him, his people, his time,
as not even he or they could have known themselves.

The projectors of the Makers of America Series
hardly could have placed him in better hands than
those of the accomplished Assistant Professor of English at Harvard.   Mr. Wendell brings to his task, his
first of the kind, an exact method habitual from
university work, and the instinct of a New Englander
steeped in the culture and traditions of the Mother
of American learning. He has had recourse to the
diaries and other MSS., largely unpublished, held by
Historical and Antiquarian Societies, and to those in
private keeping. It is greatly to be regretted that
the outcome is restricted to the narrow limits of a
volume in the present "series." What we obtain
makes it probable that, if given fuller scope, the
author would have produced a very notable biography.
As it is, Dr. Mather was not without wisdom in his
careful prevision for the illumination of after-cen-

turies, that the annals and relics of so forceful a being might not perish from among men.

With respect to Mather's share in the witchcraft tragedies of 1692, and his homicidal belief in the activity of Satan and his fiends throughout New England at that time,—as set forth in the " Magnalia " and " Perentator " and the diaries,—Professor Wendell has ideas which he presents briefly but with much effect. These are not at all inconsonant with the note of our closing century, or with the chances of the next century's demonstrations. They are certainly suggestive now that we are already familiar with " More Wonders of the Invisible World," which even Robert Calef, for all his cool-headed traverse of Matherian credulity, would not be able to gainsay. Our biographer not only accredits Mather with absolute honesty of conviction, but thinks there may have been scientific ground for the confused statements and charges of the " afflicted," young and old, in Salem. In the light of ancient and modern instances, and of our psychical research, he is not prepared to deny that there were at that time, and may now be, sensitives who do " hear a voice " and " see a hand " beyond ordinary hearing or seeing. He would look upon these as less developed natures, retaining the senses of archaic progenitors—senses akin to those of brute creatures whose quality of sight and hearing is certainly different from, if not finer than, our own. The latter-day psychologist and evolutionist more readily will believe that mankind is to acquire the future power of taking in what is now imperceptible

to us; that we are ever approaching the spiritual sen-
sitivity which is "all touch, all eye, all ear." The
theosophist will aver that certain adepts already have
reached that goal. But Professor Wendell, if we mistake not, is the first of historical writers to take the
view that the witchcraft declarations are not to be
repelled altogether as born of malice or delusion; that
there may be conditions all about us which are entirely within nature, yet not discoverable by the normal
perception of the average man. What he says upon
this topic is of singular interest and affords new hints
for discussion.

On the whole a graphic portraiture, largely from
his own pencil, is given of the voluminous Mather—a
Cambridge prodigy in youth, both of piety and learning, and of a disposition to exercise those attainments
for the regulation of less-favored mortals,—a disposition which possibly is even yet not without exemplars
in the places that once knew him. We see him from
first to last endowed with the Puritan second-sight,
familiar with apparitional imps and angels, ecstatic
as Swedenborg or Böhme; of implicit credulity in his
father's *Remarkable Providences,* and with an imagination so inflamed thereby that he unwittingly
became in character, though not in power, a type of
the egotist, the tyrant and the bigot. With no more
appreciation of the comic than Sewall exhibits, he
writes of himself and his surroundings with grotesque
fidelity. His present chronicler, while rarely dilating
upon the ludicrous side of his meditations, must have
chuckled now and then, if not unblessed with humor,

while leaving that so manifestly to speak for itself. But Professor Wendell usually remembers that he holds a brief for his subject, and discharges his trust becomingly.

Indeed, the distinctive result of his labor is that he has shown Cotton Mather not alone as history thus far has shown him: not merely, on the one side, as the most loquacious pedant, yet in truth most learned scholar, of his time; not merely as the egotist, the mystic, the theocrat, the promoter of the Salem trials; nor yet merely as the author of that unique, quaintly inclusive, survey of his compeers without which none can fully comprehend the early and middle colonial periods; but he has set before us a man who may in justice be absolved from the charge of obstinate bad faith and concealed recognition of terrible mistakes. He has taken us into Dr. Mather's sanctuary and patiently laid bare the chambers of his heart, wherein even his unfaltering credulity invests him with something like heroism. He has conceived of the Puritan priest as sincere to the last, as one who died a good man, going to his grave stricken but not cast down. It was " a good man," he enables the reader also to believe, " whom they buried on Copp's Hill one February day in the year 1728," just as he had rounded the sixty-fifth year of a defiantly militant pilgrimage.

XXV

JULIET'S RUNAWAY, ONCE MORE[1]

THE ignorance that knows itself, quoth the Seigneur de Montaigne, is not an absolute ignorance, and this is my one excuse for the presumption of adding even a votive pebble to the cairn which marching hosts of commentators have heaped above the embalmed dust of Shakespeare. For I long since knew that I never was and never could be his textual scholar, in the smallest degree illustrated during the evolution from Rowe and Warburton to Furness. Grateful to those who faithfully have labored to set forth the true version, I am of the laity who read it without question, for its wisdom, passion, imagination, and inexhaustible delight.

Meanwhile I take pride in our New World scholarship, and will say, in passing, that when Mr. Gosse wrote me that we did many fine things, but that we perforce must leave English literary research to those anear the rich materials treasured in the motherland, I had a fortunate rejoinder. It was a satisfaction to declare that the two most notable works of textual verification now issuing were from the American press, and edited by American scholars. I cited Pro-

[1] *Poet-Lore,* 1892. Richard G. Badger, Publisher.

fessor Child's *English and Scottish Popular Ballads* and Dr. H. H. Furness's New Variorum Edition of Shakespeare; and Mr. Gosse—a fair and sound expositor—handsomely doffed his cap to the citation.

It happened that my first youthful notion of what Shakespearian criticism meant, in its subtle painstaking, was derived from an article in *Putnam's Monthly* by one who bravely started out as "Shakespeare's Scholar"—the early signature of R. G. White. His long paper was devoted to a consideration of its title: "Who was Juliet's Runaway?" That conundrum, I believe, has haunted every one to whom it has been put. Collier forty years ago declared that far more suggestions had been made in answer than there are letters in the disputed word. I remember the sense of awe with which I pondered on Mr. White's avowal: "He who discovers the needful word for the misprint '*runawayes* eyes' . . . will secure the honorable mention of his name as long as the English language is read and spoken." What erudite humility, I thought, in his faith that "to correct a single passage in Shakespeare's text is glory enough for one man!" At that time he held a brief for the suggestion as to which he afterwards learned, when a riper "scholar," that Heath and Singer had anticipated him,—all three reading "That *Rumoures* eyes may wincke," instead of "That run-aways eyes," etc.: —in truth, a plausible conjecture. But in 1861 Mr. White had gone back to the belief of Warburton that the word as it stands is correct, and not a misprint; that it relates to Phœbus, the Sun, the god of day.

[281]

Dr. Furness, by occupying the most conspicuous part of his Appendix (to *Romeo and Juliet*) with a formidable synopsis of the guesses concerning our runaway, shows that a certain respect is still due it, as perchance the yet-to-be-solved riddle of that Sphinx the earliest misprinter.

So, then, " *can* anything new be said " concerning Juliet's runaway: at least, anything new and with a savor of plausibility? As for the newness, and presuming that Dr. Furness's collation embraces the past suggestions worth regard, it seems improbable that my own has been made before. Its claim to likelihood may appeal somewhat to those who have the poetic ear, and who have that sense which is heightened by practice of style in verse or prose.

Turn, then, to " Marlowe's mighty line,"—to *The Tragical History of Doctor Faustus,* a play written after his success with *Tamburlaine,* probably about 1588. Bear in mind that Shakespeare's first draft of *Romeo and Juliet* was written, it is believed, about 1591, and that there is no evidence that it appeared in its entirety in the printed text of 1597— which contains only a few lines of Juliet's soliloquy as put forth in the subsequent collections. Certainly it was composed at a period characterized, Verplanck says, by " the transition of Shakespeare's mind from a purely poetical to a dramatic cast of thought." There is evidence to any critic that Marlowe was Shakespeare's early dramatic " master," as far as the greater genius may be said to have had one for the rhythm of his formative period, and swiftly as he forged ahead.

The two collaborated, and the younger borrowed some of Marlowe's phrases for his after-plays, and burlesqued others. *Romeo and Juliet* was sketched out in his spring-time of echoes and impressibility with respect to feeling and style.

The experience of many a writer has been that in youth—however original his conceptions may be—he will more readily fall into the cadences and syntax of the predecessor whom he knows by heart, than commit any plagiarism with or without intent. The strongest, the most subtle, proofs of influence lie in imitation of cæsura, rhythm, structure, tone. To all this I once alluded more fully, in comparison of Tennyson with the Syracusan idyllists.

Turn, as I say, to the last scene of *Faustus,* and to the frantic soliloquy of the magician, who realizes that he has " but one bare hour to live " and then " must be damned perpetually." Consider his opening adjuration:

> *Stand still, you ever-moving spheres of heaven,*[1]
>
> *That* time may cease, and midnight never come;
> *Fair Nature's eye,* rise, rise again, and make
> Perpetual day; or let this hour be but
> A year, a month, a week, a natural day,
> *That* Faustus may repent and save his soul!
> *O lente, lente currite, noctis equi!*

Then read from the soliloquy of Juliet, *Romeo and Juliet,* iii. 2:

[1] The italics in these passages, the Latin verse excepted, are of course my own.

> *Gallop apace, you fiery-footed steeds,*
> Towards Phœbus' lodging: such a waggoner
> As Phaethon would whip you to the West,
> And bring in cloudy night immediately.—
> Spread thy close curtain, love-performing night,
> *That runaway's eyes* may wink, and Romeo
> Leap to these arms, untalk'd of and unseen.—

Now, whether right or wrong in my ensuing conjecture as to "runaway's eyes" (or, as the First Folio has it, "run-awayes eyes"), I feel assured, through both instinct and analysis, that young Shakespeare had the Faustus soliloquy by heart,—that its every phrase and cadence tingled in his own fibre when he wrote the adjuration of our impassioned and freespoken Juliet. For, look you,—over and above the rhythm and syntax, the turns of the phrases, the explicatory "That" similarly placed in both passages, —note that Juliet's demand for haste is merely the *converse* of Faustus's wild cry for postponement, just as her whole apostrophe betokens joy and rapturous expectation, and his—hopeless gloom, the recoil of fierce despair.

There are natural changes in the order. Translate Marlowe's *O lente, lente currite, noctis equi!*—

> O gently, gently foot it, steeds of night!

and you have the converse of

> Gallop apace, you fiery-footed steeds!

But to the very point. Marlowe bids *Fair Nature's eye* rise again and make perpetual day: he adjures the Sun to banish fell night and its damnations. Having chanced, then, to observe the close reflection in Shakespeare's mind of the Faustus prototype—quite as close, the instinct feels, as that which connects the Garden Tower in New York with the Giralda Tower of Seville, and equally no more a plagiarism—observing this, it is borne in upon me that he made Juliet call upon night to spread her close curtain,

> That *Nature's eye* may wink, and Romeo
> Leap to these arms, untalk'd of and unseen;

that, in other words, the Sun whose steeds she bids gallop apace, the sun which Faustus calls " Fair Nature's eye," may " wincke " for the nonce, and let the lovers " doe their amorous rights."

But if any one insists upon retaining the plural " eyes," doubting that successive misprints should occur, then I would read

> That *Nature's eyes* may wink, and Romeo—

the eyes of Nature *at night* being indubitably the stars, whose " winckeing " or twinkling [1] serves only to make darkness romantically visible, and bewrays lovers no more than would a mist of tropical fireflies.

Some experience of printing and script-reading fortifies me against the most obvious exception to

[1] The latter word, etymologically, is simply the " frequentative " of the former.

[285]

my conjecture. For if, as so many believe, "run-awayes" was a misprint, it is quite probable that the blindly-written word in the manuscript was no more like the printer's substitute than like any one of fifty others that would fill the allotted space. With Grant White, I am not troubled by the absence of a long letter in my word, to correspond with the *y* in "run-awayes." "Rumoures eyes" is not a bad guess. One might accept it, but for the cousinship of the two soliloquies. I make no account of "rude day's," "runagate's," "enemies'," "unawares," and a dozen other far-fetched guesses of prosaic scholiasts. The one claim of several is that they begin with R. But the slightest bend of the second down-stroke in the written N (Elizabethan) transforms it into R; so that "nature's" need not be debarred on that score.

The mutual likeness of the two soliloquies crops out here and there throughout them. Its most curious vagary is the fantastic, elfish sound-echo, in Juliet's speech, of the weak lines in *Faustus:*

> O soul, be chang'd into little water-drops,
> And fall into the ocean, ne'er be found!

This reappears,—the meaning apart,—in

> Give me my Romeo, and when I shall die,
> Take him and cut him out in little starres, etc.

There is good warrant for our natural faith in tradition, in the correct transmission of ancient "instances "—of saws, proverbs, nursery rhymes, of classic phrases whether scriptory or conveyed from mouth to mouth. Small thanks to an audacious bookman, like Ahrens, imperiously well equipped, who not only rewrites whole verses of Theocritus but transposes their entire succession in an idyl! Despite the undeniable, even bristling, errors in the First Folio, "runaway's eyes" does not excite my absolute scepticism; for I would not, like Warburton, White, and others, deem Phœbus the runaway, but would rather think that Juliet—all woman yet all child—applied that pretty appellation to her dainty self. To an editor who by chance was a bit of a poet, that notion might not seem half so fanciful as many of the conceits in Shakespeare's deathless apotheosis of youth, with all its efflorescence of speech and passion, its happy hapless voice and deed. But my acceptance of the word which so many censors have disallowed at last has been shaken—the argument through analogy being so convincing—by a chance comparison of Juliet's speech with its model in a play by resonant Kit Marlowe.

It used to be said that every French author owed it to himself to write one naughty book. Nowadays the maxim is reversed: he writes one virtuous book, *teste* Zola's *" Le Rêve,"* as a personal and tributary rite. Nevertheless, I piously believe it is not wholly in the same spirit that these surmises, respecting one word of all that Shakespeare left us, are confided to the reader.

[My one bit of Shakespearian comment.: I am still just as certain of my point, as Dr. Waldstein was of the origin of the marble head in the Louvre, which *did* fit shoulders of an Elgin figure in the British museum.—E. C. S., 1907.]